A New Lease of Life?

Anglican Clergy Reflect on Retirement

— EDITED BY —

TONY NEAL & LESLIE J. FRANCIS

Sacristy
Press

Sacristy Press
PO Box 612, Durham, DH1 9HT

www.sacristy.co.uk

First published in 2020 by Sacristy Press, Durham

Scripture quotations, unless otherwise stated, are from the New Revised
Standard Version Bible: Anglicized Edition, copyright © 1989, 1995
National Council of the Churches of Christ in the United States of
America. Used by permission. All rights reserved worldwide.

Every reasonable effort has been made to trace the copyright holders
of material reproduced in this book, but if any have been inadvertently
overlooked the publisher would be glad to hear from them.

Sacristy Limited, registered in England & Wales, number 7565667

British Library Cataloguing-in-Publication Data
A catalogue record for the book is available from the British Library

ISBN 978-1-78959-085-2

PREFACE

In 1976, legislation introduced clergy retirement at the age of seventy. Forty years later, we considered that the time was right to explore how clergy retirement may be impacting the lives of individual clergymen and clergywomen and may be affecting the life of the Church. Our first enquiry comprised a questionnaire survey among diocesan bishops. We were grateful to those bishops who responded. Then we wanted to explore the perceptions and experiences of retired clergy themselves. Given the absence of a serious research literature on this matter we decided that the most effective starting point would be to listen to the narrative stories of individual clergy who had moved into retirement. Recognizing broad diversity among retired clergy, we wanted to listen to retired clergymen and to retired clergywomen, to those who had served in stipendiary ministry and to those who had served in self-supporting ministry, to those who had served in ordained ministry for close on the full forty years, and those who had been ordained later in life.

Our initiative was to compile and to edit the collection of narratives, but the real credit goes to our colleagues who have been willing to tell their individual stories with openness and with integrity. We offered each of our colleagues the cloak of anonymity, but none wanted to accept that offer. From these individual narratives some clear themes emerge that touch on matters of theological, ecclesiological, pastoral, and missiological significance. In raising these matters, we invite the Church to listen and to take them seriously. Beginning with narrative enquiry, we commend the value of building on this initial study with a well-designed quantitative survey.

In preparing this book for publication we wish to place on record our gratitude to Emma Eccles for her patient and skilful work on shaping the manuscript, to Judith Muskell for her careful attention to proofreading, and to Natalie Watson for her professional editorial oversight.

Tony Neal and Leslie J. Francis
Easter 2019

CONTENTS

Preface iii

Introduction 1

1. Profiling Religiously Engaged Retired Clergy *(Leslie J. Francis)* ... 9
2. What is Retirement? *(Brian McQuillen)* 21
3. Retirement or Bereavement? *(Katy Morgan)* 31
4. Vocation versus Retirement *(Judy Howard)* 41
5. An Early Retirement? *(John Eatock)* 51
6. And some have retirement thrust upon them *(Peter Knibbs)* 63
7. A Substitute Priest? *(David Jennings)* 75
8. Mission, Spiritual Direction, and Research *(John Holmes)*....... 85
9. Hospital Chaplaincy and Mentoring *(Tony Neal)* 95
10. Mission Partners and the Retired Clergy Association
    (David Phypers) 107
11. Finding a Home and Making a Life *(Tim Newcombe)* 115
12. The Priest as Night-soil Man: Reflecting on Outsidedness
    (David Peel).. 129
13. We shall not cease from exploration *(Nancy Johnson)* 145
14. Being Positive and Realistic *(Pat Robson)*.................. 155
15. Homecoming *(Anthony Phillips)* 167
16. Reflecting on the Narratives *(David S. Walker)*.............. 179

INTRODUCTION

Tony Neal and Leslie J. Francis

When Leslie J. Francis (1985) undertook his research into the life and ministry of the Church of England throughout one rural diocese during the early 1980s, the impact of legislation to introduce compulsory retirement from beneficed livings at the age of seventy was only just beginning to filter through. While much of *Rural Anglicanism* was based on statistical profiles, chapter 12 turned attention to the insights generated by participant observers who set out to attend all twenty-four church services held in one rural deanery on the third Sunday in May. Quite incidentally, the participant observers met and fell into conversation with two active parish priests who would by today's standards have been long retired. One of these priests had already been serving his Tractarian parish for over fifty years. He smiled that he was already over seventy when the retirement legislation came into force, so clearly that was irrelevant for him. Another of these priests had been inducted into a quiet rural benefice of two churches at the age of sixty-five during the late 1960s. He saw this as his "last living" and had thrown himself energetically into introducing charismatic worship to a traditional village church.

CLERGY RETIREMENT

The 1976 legislation introducing clergy retirement at the age of seventy has now worked its way through the Church of England and has helped both to modernize and to professionalize the Church. The impact, however, has been seen on the quality of life experienced by aging clergy, on the costs of pension provision, and on the changing balance between the numbers of stipendiary clergy and the numbers of retired clergy.

Statistics published by the Church of England in 2019 show that in 2018 there were 7,700 stipendiary clergy (2,250 women and 5,450 men), 2,540 NSM clergy (1,250 women and 1,290 men), 380 OLM clergy (220 women and 160 men), and 7,230 clergy holding PTO/LTO recognition to officiate (1,800 women and 5,430 men). Most of those holding permission to officiate may well be retired clergy, although the proportion is not specified. Other retired clergy may be included within the NSM category (Church of England, 2019, p. 9). The trend statistics show is a slight fall in stipendiary clergy from 8,797 in 2014 to 7,700 in 2018 a slight fall in NSM clergy from 2,830 in 2014 to 2,540 in 2016, and a fall in OLM clergy from 480 in 2014 to 380 in 2018. At the same time there has been a slight rise in clergy holding PTO/LTO from 6,450 in 2014 to 7,230 in 2018.

In spite of their growing number, surprisingly little attention or research has been given to the experiences and expectations of retired clergy within the context of the Church of England today. This is surprising for both theological and pragmatic reasons.

Theologically, ordination within the Church of England still appears to be something that involves life-long commitment. While individual priests may retire from the active exercise of priestly ministry, it is not so readily assumed that they will have retired from priestly orders. Both the privileges and the obligations incurred by episcopal ordination remain for life. While properly subject to episcopal licence, the retired priest retains the authority to preside at eucharist and to pronounce absolution for the penitent. The retired priest remains a public witness to the priestly presence of the Church within society. The retired priest, remaining faithful to ordination vows, remains committed to a pattern of prayer, to the study of scripture, and to a way of life modelled on the example of Christ. All these expectations are grounded in the ordinal of 1662 and reaffirmed by subsequent revision of the ordinal.

Pragmatically, the very fact that many retired clergy hold permission to officiate underscores the anecdotal observation regarding the key contributions made by retired clergy to maintaining the regular rhythm of church services, perhaps especially within rural dioceses. However, the effective ministries of retired clergy go well beyond liturgical provision. For example, our recent enquiry conducted among diocesan bishops identified examples of retired clergy contributing to the life of the Church in a variety of other ways, including serving as mentors to younger clergy, acting as interim ministers in vacant parishes, serving as the local minister for a local congregation within a multi-church benefice, and serving as rural deans (see Neal, Francis and McKenna, 2017).

The diocesan bishops who spoke in our survey about the important contribution being made by retired clergy within their dioceses also voiced two notes of caution. The first note of caution concerned the danger of retired clergy losing touch with the developing shape of ministry within a constantly changing Church. Several of the participating bishops suggested that, after a certain period of retirement, retired clergy may become less effective and less helpful, perhaps especially in the field of mentoring younger colleagues. This caveat may highlight the need for dioceses that encourage the effective deployment of retired clergy to ensure that such retired clergy are kept fully involved with the diocesan programmes of continuing ministerial education and continuing ministerial development.

The second note of caution concerned the danger that, if the Church were to rely too heavily on the deployment of retired clergy, this may detract from dealing with the long-term strategic problem of planning for sustainable ministry into the future. This caveat highlights the need for dioceses that encourage the effective deployment of retired clergy to do so within the context of a responsible ongoing audit of ministry needs and ministry resources, involving an integrated vision for retired clergy alongside stipendiary clergy, other forms of ordained ministry, and forms of authorized (and unauthorized) lay ministry.

Our previous study set out to explore how diocesan bishops viewed the contributions that retired clergy were making within their dioceses. Clearly such a study needs to be complemented by listening to the voices of retired clergy themselves, and that is what the present book sets out to do.

LISTENING TO RETIRED CLERGY

Chapter 1 sets the scene by drawing on a survey that attracted responses from 784 religiously engaged retired clergy over the age of fifty-nine years and living in England, Ireland, Scotland, and Wales. This quantitative survey allowed the experiences, practices, and attitudes of three groups of retired clergy to be compared: those in their sixties, those in their seventies, and those aged eighty and over.

Following on from this quantitative survey, fourteen retired clergy accepted our invitation to "tell their story", and they do so with openness, honesty, and integrity. A qualitative study of this nature makes no pretence of offering a representative survey of clergy opinions, but what it does achieve is to offer a variety of perspectives, which speak into the joy and into the pain offered by the opportunities and challenges presented by retirement, after a time of service in active ordained ministry.

In chapter 2, Brian McQuillen reflects on "What is retirement?" Having been ordained in 1976 (the year in which the Church of England passed the measure requiring priests to retire at the age of seventy), Brian retired in 2011. He reflects on the changing face of the Church of England and what it means to be a retired priest in today's world and in today's Church. He argues that a priest retires from a specific function or specific post, but not from priesthood itself.

In chapter 3, Katy Morgan describes how she experienced retirement from stipendiary parish ministry as bereavement. Katy had worked as a primary school teacher before being ordained deacon in 1996. She made history as the first woman priest to serve in the parish in which her father had served before her. For Katy retirement was a four-fold bereavement. She had lost: her job to which she had been called and for which she had been trained; her daily contact with the people among whom she had been working, and living; her home established within the parish; and much of her past as she emptied the rectory to live in a much smaller house.

In chapter 4, Judy Howard discusses how she redefined her sense of vocation in retirement. She had been ordained deacon in 2001 into self-supporting ministry. She remained living in her own home and commuted eleven miles to the parish in which she served for nine years, first as curate and then as associate priest. Then after retirement she struggled to re-enter her own parish church in which her vocation had been formed. The best that could be offered was going back on the coffee rota, and she wept. Then in retirement she developed her home to shape a vocation of monastic hospitality.

In chapter 5, John Eatock describes his experience of choosing "early retirement". He had been ordained deacon in 1970 and in 1992 (aged forty-seven) resigned from his incumbency to pursue a future as a self-supporting priest engaged as a counsellor and psychotherapist. From that point the Church counted him among "retired clergy". He continued to see his work as fulfilling priestly vocation, but largely unrecognized by the Church. Now retired from his career as a counsellor and psychotherapist, the Church is beginning to recognize his contribution to the pastoral care of clergy.

In chapter 6, Peter Knibbs discusses the experience of having "early retirement" thrust on him through ill health. He had been ordained into self-supporting ministry and had worked in the National Health Service for thirty-three years before transferring to stipendiary ministry. In his late fifties Peter suffered a heart attack. In this chapter he reflects on the theological challenges and practical opportunities arising from this disruption to his anticipated trajectory.

In chapter 7, David Jennings reflects on the identity crisis that came with retirement. He had been ordained deacon in 1974 and retired in 2014. In retirement he has continued to serve as canon theologian at Leicester Cathedral, and undertook a significant interim ministry within a difficult parish. He reflects on the crisis of identity that comes with retirement, on the impact of moving away from friends, and on the need for care with managing occasional fees and expenses. He shapes a vision for the place of retired clergy within a changing Church.

In chapter 8, John Holmes describes how retirement provided new opportunities and new directions for his sense of vocation. He had been ordained in 1966 and has served his ministry in the Dioceses of Ripon and Wakefield, as curate, vicar, rural dean, diocesan missioner, and canon missioner. He retired in 2007. In retirement he engaged within the fields of mission, spiritual direction, and mentoring. He also led a stream of the

Church of England's Church Growth Research Programme concerning cathedrals and greater churches.

In chapter 9, Tony Neal considers how retirement had opened up for him new opportunities both to reflect on ministry and to engage with ministry in new ways. He had been ordained deacon in 1968 and moved to the Diocese of Truro in 1981. He retired in 2006. Immediately before retirement he had established a Team Ministry and served as chair of the House of Clergy. He tells an honest tale of finding a small house for retirement, engaging in some serious academic study, and serving as part-time hospital chaplain, before responding to the call to re-engage with part-time parochial ministry, serving as associate priest in a cluster of eight rural churches, and as mentor to a rector serving his first incumbency.

In chapter 10, David Phypers discusses how retirement gave him opportunities to engage with an overseas mission agency and to serve local voluntary organizations, in spite of financial pressures. In 1985, he had retired from school teaching on health grounds, having been ordained deacon in 1978 as a self-supporting minister. In 1988 he accepted the stipendiary post as priest-in-charge of two small villages. At that point he made his first mistake. He sold his house. David retired in 2007 and now lives in a house provided by the Pensions Board that takes 30 per cent of the joint gross income of him and his wife. In retirement David has been very active supporting CMS Mission Partners in Nepal, serving as treasurer for two local voluntary organizations, and serving as treasurer of the Retired Clergy Association of the Church of England.

In chapter 11, Tim Newcombe shares the experience of being a single gay priest making a fresh life for himself, a fresh life in the Church, and a fresh life in the community. He had been ordained deacon in 1976 and retired after thirty-seven years in full-time stipendiary service. Twelve years earlier he had been challenged by a couple of his parishioners to invest in a house for retirement, and they had helped him to do precisely that. Now in retirement he reflects on his experiences as a single gay priest in the Church of England. The immediate experience of retirement was one of pain and loss, especially on Sundays. But from these painful beginnings Tim tells the creative experience of making a life, getting a life in the Church, and getting a life in the community.

In chapter 12, David Peel, who had been ordained deacon in 1976 and who had retired at the age of seventy in 2012, reflects on a ministry inspired by a passion for working among the poor, the powerless, the dispossessed, and the disadvantaged. He spent most of his ministry serving within the Church, but outside the Church of England's structure. Now having retired, David remains actively engaged in broadly the same spheres of ministry. In particular he speaks of his involvement with prisons, his involvement with cathedral chaplaincy, and his involvement with The International Metropolitan Community Church, founded to serve people who are gay, transgendered, or otherwise perceived as sexually "different". David describes himself as "a priest in the Church of England who happens to have been born gay".

In chapter 13, Nancy Johnson reflects on the wisdom that comes with aging. She had been ordained deacon in 2002 in her fifties, having earlier in life tested her vocation in the novitiate of The Sisters of the Love of God in Oxford, and having taught at Grey Coat Hospital in Westminster with its close links to Westminster Abbey. Her ministry was served in hospital chaplaincy, continuing to live in her own home with her husband. Nancy retired in 2010. In retirement Nancy has been learning about handing responsibilities over to others and about the quality of wisdom that used to be associated with the elderly. She is aware that the future will hold significant losses. There will be bereavements as family and friends die, and she will have to learn to live with loss. Learning to face up to this with courage and faith is one of the tasks ahead.

In chapter 14, Pat Robson speaks openly and positively about facing death. Following her divorce, Pat moved to Cornwall (with her natural son, her adopted son, and a huge Airedale) to take up a teaching post in a boys' grammar school. She was ordained deacon in 1987, and three years later took over running a large country parish. Pat retired in 2005. Now in retirement Pat remains very active within the charity she started twenty-five years ago working with children in Romania (visiting Romania four times a year) and works as a self-employed study tutor supporting university students with special needs in order to help fund her work in Romania. Now seventy-five years old, Nancy talks openly about death: "I want a good death. I don't want to be afraid and so I know I must prepare carefully."

In chapter 15, Anthony Phillips reflects at the approach of his eightieth birthday on the final homecoming to which life inevitably moves. He had been ordained deacon in 1966 and served his curacy in a new church on a Cambridge housing estate. From there he was appointed to an academic and pastoral post at Trinity Hall, Cambridge and subsequently to a post at St John's College, Oxford. Then after ten years as Head of The King's School, Canterbury he retired at the age of sixty. Coming back home to retire in Cornwall (where for many years he had been canon theologian) had given Anthony good opportunities for finding ministry and taking up new interests in retirement. As his eightieth birthday approached, Anthony faced exile from Cornwall for a second time to move closer to his daughter in Oxford and to prepare for the final homecoming.

Our hope is that the richness and variety of these fourteen voices will stimulate others to build on the foundations provided by our investigation, both to invest in further research in this field and to think more strategically about the theological and pragmatic implications for a Church that has more clergy living on pensions than on stipends.

REFERENCES

Church of England (2019), *Ministry Statistics 2018*, London: Research and Statistics.

Francis, L. J. (1985), *Rural Anglicanism: A Future for Young Christians?* London: Collins Liturgical Publications.

Neal, T., Francis, L. J., & McKenna, U. (2017), "A survey on mentoring, first incumbency, and the role of retired clergy: Listening to bishops", *Rural Theology* 15, pp. 39–47.

1. PROFILING RELIGIOUSLY ENGAGED RETIRED CLERGY

Leslie J. Francis

The survey included in the *Church Times* in 2013 attracted responses from 784 retired clergy over the age of fifty-nine years and living in England, Ireland, Scotland, and Wales (see further, Village, 2018). These are clearly retired clergy who have remained significantly engaged with church life and who have wished to stay up to date with church news by reading a quality church newspaper. A further nine clergy who had retired before the age of sixty were not included in the analysis on the grounds that early retirement in itself represents a special category. The aim of the present study is to look in depth at the responses to the survey by those retired clergy over the age of fifty-nine. Here are unique windows into who religiously engaged retired clergy really are, how much they engage in religious practices and activities, what they believe about God and the Church, and how they feel about the churches and congregations to which they continue to relate. Drawing on the data provided by the *Church Times* survey, the following analyses concentrate on two main areas. The first offers a demographic profile and the second offers an attitudinal profile.

DEMOGRAPHIC PROFILE

Sex

Men still far outnumber women among those religiously engaged retired clergy. The participants included 675 men (86 per cent) compared with 109 women (14 per cent). This is unsurprising given that women were first ordained into the diaconate within the Church of England in 1987 and into the priesthood in 1994 (see Francis & Robbins, 1999).

Age

The largest age group of these religiously engaged retired clergy comprised clergy in their seventies (N = 367, 47 per cent), with 183 in their sixties (23 per cent) and 234 aged eighty or over (30 per cent). While 16 per cent of religiously engaged retired clergy in their sixties were women, the proportions fell to 15 per cent among those in their seventies and to 10 per cent among those in their eighties or older.

Countries of residence

The large majority of religiously engaged retired clergy over all three age groups were living in England (92 per cent), with 5 per cent in Wales, 2 per cent in Scotland, and 1 per cent in Ireland.

Areas of residence

Retiring to the countryside is most attractive to religiously engaged retired clergy in their sixties (48 per cent), but the proportions drop to 40 per cent in their seventies and to 33 per cent in their eighties or older. With increasing age religiously engaged retired clergy tend to migrate more to urban and to suburban areas.

Marital status

Similar proportions of religiously engaged retired clergy within the three age bands were single: 10 per cent in their sixties, 12 per cent in their seventies, and 12 per cent in their eighties or older. The proportion of those who were married (or remarried) declined over the three age categories: 81 per cent in their sixties, 75 per cent in their seventies, and 63 per cent in their eighties or older. The proportion of those who were widowed inevitably increased over the three age categories: 4 per cent in their sixties, 9 per cent in their seventies, and 24 per cent in their eighties or older. A small number were separated or divorced: 3 per cent in their sixties, 2 per cent in their seventies, and 1 per cent in their eighties or older; and an even smaller number were in civil partnerships: 1 per cent in their sixties and fewer than 1 per cent in their seventies or in their eighties and older.

Church attendance

Church attendance remained high among these religiously engaged retired clergy. Weekly attendance was reported by 90 per cent of those in their sixties, 95 per cent of those in their seventies, and 93 per cent of those in their eighties and over. Many of these religiously engaged retired clergy reported multiple attendances each week: 28 per cent in their sixties, 34 per cent in their seventies, and 34 per cent in their eighties or older.

Cathedral attendance

Cathedrals were quite attractive to religiously engaged retired clergy: 6 per cent of those in their sixties and seventies saw the cathedral as their main place of Sunday worship, with the proportion rising to 10 per cent of those in their eighties or older. Cathedrals were seen as places of regular weekday worship by between 6 per cent and 7 per cent of all three age groups. Many more religiously engaged retired clergy attended cathedrals for special occasions: 53 per cent in their sixties, 55 per cent in their seventies, and 48 per cent in their eighties or older.

Prayer and Bible reading

Daily reading from the Bible was maintained by 64 per cent of religiously engaged retired clergy in their sixties, by 71 per cent in their seventies, and by 77 per cent in their eighties or older. Daily prayer was maintained by 85 per cent of religiously engaged retired clergy in their sixties, by 87 per cent in their seventies, and by 92 per cent in their eighties or older.

ATTITUDINAL PROFILE

Within the *Church Times* survey an attitudinal profile of religiously engaged retired clergy was generated by a series of short, focused statements to which they were invited to respond on a simple five-point scale: agree strongly, agree, not certain, disagree, and disagree strongly. An example item reads like this:

> I feel a strong sense of belonging to my church. AS A NC D DS

In the following analyses the agree strongly and the agree responses have been added together to provide a single measure of assent.

Because it was thought likely that responses to some of these statements might change with age, the responses to each item were calculated separately for the three age groups: those in their sixties, those in their seventies, and those aged eighty or older.

From the range of themes explored in the *Church Times* survey the following analyses report on twelve themes: sense of belonging, sense of satisfaction with worship, building for the future, spiritual practices, ancient and modern preferences in worship, believing the creeds, believing the Bible, attitudes toward other faiths, sex and marriage, homosexuality, ordination of homosexuals, and divorce and remarriage.

Sense of belonging

The four items designed to gauge the sense of belonging demonstrate that religiously engaged retired clergy in their sixties feel quite closely involved with their church. Four out of every five say that they feel a strong sense of belonging to their church (81 per cent). Two out of every three say that their church is important for their social life (65 per cent), and that members of their church care deeply for one another (65 per cent). Almost half say that they turn to fellow members of their church when they need help (47 per cent).

This close sense of belonging increases as religiously engaged retired clergy grow older. While 81 per cent of those in their sixties feel a strong sense of belonging to their church, the proportions rise to 88 per cent of those in their seventies, and to 96 per cent of those in their eighties or older. While 65 per cent of those in their sixties feel that their church is important for their social life, the proportions rise to 75 per cent of those in their seventies, and to 83 per cent of those in their eighties and older. While 65 per cent of those in their sixties feel that members of their church care deeply for one another, the proportions rise to 73 per cent of those in their seventies, and to 78 per cent of those in their eighties and older. While 47 per cent of those in their sixties turn to fellow members of their church when they need help, the proportions rise to 58 per cent of those in their seventies, and to 63 per cent of those in their eighties or older.

Sense of satisfaction with worship

The two positive items designed to gauge the sense of satisfaction with worship demonstrate that six out of every ten religiously engaged retired clergy in their sixties feel that their church meets their spiritual needs (61 per cent), and that seven out of ten feel that the worship in their church connects to their daily life (70 per cent). These positive evaluations increase as religiously engaged retired clergy grow older. While 61 per cent of those in their sixties feel that their church meets their spiritual needs, the proportions rise to 66 per cent of those in their seventies, and to 72 per cent of those in their eighties or older. While 70 per cent of those in their sixties feel that the worship in their church connects to their daily life, the proportions rise to 73 per cent of those in their seventies, and to 78 per cent of those in their eighties or older.

The first negative item in this section demonstrates that 13 per cent of religiously engaged retired clergy in their sixties feel that the Sunday worship in their church is usually boring, but this proportion falls to 8 per cent among those in their seventies, and to 4 per cent among those in their eighties or older. The second negative item in this section demonstrates that 19 per cent of religiously engaged retired clergy in their sixties feel that they have too little control over the running of their church, and this proportion increases to 20 per cent among those in their seventies, and to 34 per cent among those in their eighties or older.

Building for the future

Overall, religiously engaged retired clergy remain positive about their own faith. Around three quarters of them feel that they are still growing in their Christian faith: 77 per cent in their sixties, 72 per cent in their seventies, and 73 per cent in their eighties or older. Moreover, as they grow older, so their attendance at their church increases. Thus, 18 per cent of those in their sixties say that they are going to their church more regularly, and the proportion increases to 22 per cent in their seventies, and to 33 per cent in their eighties or older.

Over a quarter of religiously engaged retired clergy often invite other people to come to their church: 26 per cent of those in their sixties, 29 per cent in their seventies, and 29 per cent in their eighties or older. These clergy are actively trying to build up local congregations. Around two in every five are in churches where they feel there is hope for growth. Thus, 41 per cent of those in their sixties, and 41 per cent of those in their seventies think that the membership of their church will grow in the next twelve months, although the proportion drops to 34 per cent among those in their eighties or older.

Spiritual practices

Retirement may challenge clergy to rethink and to retune spiritual practices that had become so embedded within their professional ministry. The four items in this section explored prayer and Bible reading, both of which may be solitary or communal activities, experienced alone or with others. What happens to these practices in retirement? The data demonstrate that reading the Bible and prayer remain core to religiously engaged retired clergy. Thus, between 90 per cent and 95 per cent of the three age groups affirm that they are helped in their faith by reading the Bible, and between 90 per cent and 92 per cent of the three age groups affirm that they are helped in their faith by praying by themselves. Bible study groups and prayer groups remain important to around half of religiously engaged retired clergy. Thus, between 49 per cent and 52 per cent of the three age groups affirm that they are helped in their faith by Bible study groups, and between 44 per cent and 47 per cent of the three age groups affirm that they are helped in their faith by prayer groups.

Ancient and modern

Retired clergy now in their seventies or eighties may have grown up with a faith shaped by the *Book of Common Prayer* (or the 1928 Prayer Book) and the established hymnody of *Hymns Ancient and Modern*. To what extent is their faith today still resourced by more traditional forms of worship? Among religiously engaged retired clergy in their sixties, 64 per cent say that they are helped in their faith by traditional services, compared with 51 per cent who say that they are helped in their faith by new forms of services. The proportion helped by traditional forms of services rises to 72 per cent in their seventies, and to 84 per cent in their eighties or older. Among religiously engaged retired clergy in their sixties, 73 per cent say that they are helped in their faith by traditional hymns, compared with 62 per cent who say that they are helped in their faith by new hymns/songs. The proportion helped by traditional hymns rises to 80 per cent in their seventies, and to 85 per cent in their eighties or older.

Believing the creeds

The four items in the survey designed to assess orthodox belief in the creed referred to the virgin birth of Jesus, to the physical resurrection of Jesus, to heaven, and to hell. Around three quarters of religiously engaged retired clergy in their sixties affirm belief that Jesus rose physically from the dead (73 per cent). The proportion rose slightly to 76 per cent in their seventies, and to 79 per cent in their eighties or older. Around half of religiously engaged retired clergy in their sixties affirm belief that Jesus' birth was a virgin birth (49 per cent). The proportions rise significantly to 61 per cent in their seventies, and to 65 per cent in their eighties or older. Belief in heaven or hell remains fairly constant across the three age groups. Thus, 81 per cent of religiously engaged retired clergy in their sixties, 81 per cent in their seventies, and 83 per cent in their eighties or older believe that heaven really exists. About half the number believe that hell really exists: 40 per cent in their sixties, 38 per cent in their seventies, and 43 per cent in their eighties or older.

Believing the Bible

Retired clergy in today's church are likely to have been shaped by a critical approach to the Bible. So what do they believe about the Bible? Three statements in this section of the survey explored aspects of biblical truth. The data show that four out of five religiously engaged retired clergy believe that the Bible contains truth, but it is not always true: 79 per cent in their sixties, 80 per cent in their seventies, and 83 per cent in their eighties or older. Three out of five believe that people who wrote the Bible created stories to explain things they did not understand: 63 per cent in their sixties, 60 per cent in their seventies, and 62 per cent in their eighties or older. Three out of five believe that science shows that some things in the Bible cannot have happened: 62 per cent in their sixties, 66 per cent in their seventies, and 64 per cent in their eighties or older.

The fourth statement in this section explored understanding of the Johannine narrative concerning the wedding at Cana of Galilee. Half of religiously engaged retired clergy in their sixties believe that Jesus really turned the water into wine (50 per cent), and the proportion rises to 53 per cent in their seventies, and to 59 per cent in their eighties or older.

Attitudes toward other faiths

Interfaith dialogue and attitudes toward other faiths have moved a considerable distance during the lifetime of clergy who are now retired. Two statements in this section of the survey illustrate how attitudes differ among the three age groups of religiously engaged retired clergy. Just over one third of religiously engaged retired clergy in their sixties believe that

Christianity is the only true religion (36 per cent), and the proportion rises to 45 per cent in their seventies, and to 55 per cent in their eighties or over. Three quarters of religiously engaged retired clergy in their sixties (75 per cent) and in their seventies (75 per cent) believe that Christians can learn about God from the writings of other faiths, but the proportion falls to 65 per cent in their eighties or older.

Sex and marriage

Attitudes toward sex and marriage have undergone considerable revision, both within society at large and within the Church, during the lifetime of clergy who are now retired. The data show that there are marked differences within the three age groups of religiously engaged retired clergy. Around a quarter of religiously engaged retired clergy in their sixties believe that it is wrong for men and women to have sex before marriage (23 per cent), but the proportion rises to 33 per cent in their seventies, and to 41 per cent in their eighties or older. A third of religiously engaged retired clergy in their sixties (34 per cent) and in their seventies (34 per cent) believe that it is alright for a couple to live together without intending to get married, but the proportion falls to 24 per cent in their eighties or older. A quarter of religiously engaged retired clergy in their sixties (26 per cent) and in their seventies (24 per cent) believe that it is a good idea for couples who intend to get married to live together first, but the proportion falls to 19 per cent in their eighties or older.

Homosexuality

Attitudes toward homosexuality have also undergone considerable revision, both within society at large and within the Church, during the lifetime of clergy who are now retired. The data show that there are marked differences within the three age groups of religiously engaged retired clergy. Around a quarter of religiously engaged retired clergy in their sixties believe that it is wrong for people of the same gender to have sex (24 per cent), and the proportion rises to 33 per cent in their seventies, and to 39 per cent in their eighties or older. Two-fifths of religiously engaged retired clergy in their sixties approve of homosexual couples being married in church (40 per cent), but the proportion falls to 28 per cent in their seventies, and to 21 per cent in their eighties or older. Seven out of every ten religiously engaged retired clergy in their sixties approve of homosexual couples receiving a blessing in church (70 per cent), but the proportion falls to 65 per cent in their seventies, and to 61 per cent in their eighties or older.

Ordination of homosexuals

Attitudes toward homosexuality have come into particularly clear focus within the Church of England in relation to ordination to priesthood and to episcopacy. The data show that attitudes in this area are age-related. Over half of religiously engaged retired clergy in their sixties (56 per cent) and in their seventies (55 per cent) are in favour of the ordination of practising homosexuals as priests, but the proportion falls to 46 per cent among those in their eighties or older. The same proportion of religiously engaged retired clergy in their sixties are in favour of the ordination of practising homosexuals as bishops (57 per cent), but the proportion falls more sharply to 50 per cent in their seventies, and to 39 per cent in their eighties or older. Overall, there is greater acceptance of the ordination of celibate homosexuals as priests, but the proportion still declines with age. Thus, 87 per cent of religiously engaged retired clergy in their sixties are in favour of the ordination of celibate homosexuals as priests, and the proportions fall to 84 per cent in their seventies, and to 75 per cent in their eighties or older. Similarly, 86 per cent of religiously engaged retired clergy in their sixties are in favour of the ordination of celibate homosexuals as bishops, and the proportions fall to 82 per cent in their seventies, and to 76 per cent in their eighties or older.

Divorce and remarriage

Attitudes toward divorce and remarriage have undergone considerable revision, both within society at large and within the Church, during the lifetime of clergy who are now retired. The data show that there are marked differences within the three age groups of retired clergy. Almost nine out of every ten religiously engaged retired clergy in their sixties are in favour of divorced people being married in church (88 per cent), but the proportion falls to 80 per cent in their seventies, and to 68 per cent in their eighties or older. A little over eight out of every ten religiously engaged retired clergy in their sixties are in favour of divorced and remarried priests (82 per cent), but the proportion falls to 81 per cent in their seventies, and to 63 per cent in their eighties or older. There is less support for divorced and remarried bishops than for divorced and remarried priests. Almost eight out of every ten religiously engaged retired clergy in their sixties are in favour of divorced and remarried bishops (78 per cent), and the proportion falls to 73 per cent in their seventies, and to 55 per cent in their eighties or older.

CONCLUSION

This chapter has opened unique windows into who religiously engaged retired clergy really are, what they believe about God and the Church, and how they feel about the churches and congregations to which they continue to be related. This demographic profile and attitudinal profile has been made possible by drawing on a survey included in the *Church Times* in 2013 in which 784 retired clergy (over the age of fifty-nine years and living in England, Ireland, Scotland, and Wales) submitted full responses. In some ways this is a strong sample on which to build. It is strong because it gives a good number of responses from a well-defined population, namely readers of the *Church Times*: we chose to style this sample as representing religiously engaged retired clergy. At the same time, a sample of this nature also has recognized limitations. The *Church Times* is not the only quality church newspaper accessed by Anglican clergy. Alongside the *Church Times*, the *Church of England Newspaper* may access a somewhat more Evangelical constituency of religiously engaged retired clergy. There are also other retired clergy who for a variety of reasons may not regularly access the church press.

While the present study offers the best windows currently available into the demographic profile and attitudinal profile of retired clergy, there are good reasons for hypothesizing both academic and practical benefits from undertaking a wider and systematic survey of retired clergy, including those who have retired from stipendiary ministry and those who have retired from self-supporting ministry, embracing both the religiously engaged and the religiously disengaged. From an academic perspective, research of this nature should contribute to two developing bodies of knowledge: one concerned with the psychology of religious formation, and the other concerned with the connections between religion and aging. From a practical perspective, research of this nature should enable the Church to release more fully the potential of retired clergy to contribute to the mission and ministry of the many parish churches that draw on the resources of retired clergy. It should also enable the Church to fulfil more adequately the duty of care both to religiously engaged and to religiously disengaged retired clergy.

While quantitative research of the kind facilitated by the *Church Times* survey can provide rich insights into broader trends and patterns among retired clergy, there are enormous benefits in complementary studies by qualitative research that allow the distinctive voices of individual retired clergy to be heard. The remaining chapters of this book do precisely that.

REFERENCES

Church of England (2017), *Ministry Statistics 2016*, London: Research and Statistics.

Francis, L. J. & Robbins, M. (1999), *The Long Diaconate: 1987–1994*, Leominster: Gracewing.

Village, A. (2018), *The Church of England in the First Decade of the Twenty-first Century: Findings from the Church Times Surveys*, New York: Palgrave Macmillan.

2. WHAT IS RETIREMENT?

Brian McQuillen

In 1976 the General Synod of the Church of England passed a measure requiring all priests to retire at the age of seventy. When most of the men employed at that time looked forward to retiring at sixty-five, it must have been acknowledged that Anglican priests were made of a stronger constitution or simply sterner stuff. The proposers of such a legal measure were possibly concerned at the number of very elderly clergy over the age of seventy who were not capable of fulfilling, or perhaps unwilling to fulfil, the full requirements of their ministry. Up until that year a priest, always male, could look forward to ending his ministry in office, dying with a prayer book in one hand, pipe in the other, and a grieving black Labrador recumbent on the vicarage croquet lawn.

A CHANGING CHURCH

I was ordained in Birmingham Cathedral at Petertide, also in 1976, on the hottest day of the year, wearing little under my thick woollen cassock and sweating profusely in the heat and with nerves. It was a prophetic preparation for things to come. Like all my colleagues at that time I expected to be trained in two parishes as a curate, before looking forward in eager anticipation to being responsible for my own (single) parish, complete with large home, the benefits of a regular stipend, and the security of knowing that the Church of England would always look after me until exhausted after a lifetime's ministry, I would simply roll over and collapse into my grave.

During my forty years in parochial ministry, the Church of England has changed almost out of all recognition. Although in essence parochial ministry has changed little, and the methodology of the Church of England has remained little altered, the demands on a parish priest's time and energy have increased. There are more parishes in groups and clusters to manage and serve, with the added and more complex responsibility of more church buildings, halls, and people to care for. Consequently, there is less clergy relaxation and more stress, leading to less time for reading and theological reflection. Sadly, regular disciplined prayer time often seems squeezed into a tight corner. The Church generally has been very slow in providing ordered support for parish priests who minister on their own. Thankfully attempts are being made to rectify this shortcoming.

During the past forty years other positive changes have evolved too. In our liturgy, besides the continuing use of the *Book of Common Prayer* (both 1662 and 1928), *Series 3* came to an end in 1980 with the introduction of *The Alternative Service Book 1980*, and then *Common Worship* in 2000. The mid-morning Parish Communion evolved with the decline in Mattins, and there are now fewer churches offering Evening Prayer. There has been an explosion in evangelism with new, adventurous teaching of the gospel and inspirational projects for children and young people. Women priests and bishops have added a new, positive dimension to ministry, making a wonderful contribution to the needs of our world and Church, and lay people are more involved in worship and decision-making. Yet it is ironic that priests in retirement are needed more than ever.

DOES A PRIEST REALLY RETIRE?

This latter point is worth noting. The term "retirement" is misleading for a priest approaching the end of full-time ministry. A Member of Parliament may apply for the Chiltern Hundreds, a worker may "hang up one's hatchet" or be "put out to pasture", and a sailor may "swallow the anchor". A priest may "retire" from a particular type or style of ministry, from an appointment or office, but not from priesthood. In ordaining a person "priest" the Church acknowledges that they have been called by

God and therefore, unless found guilty of some crime or misdemeanour, cannot become a "non-priest". In fact, it is legally impossible for a priest personally to resign from holy orders, for then the Church would be formally acknowledging that it has been mistaken and that the ordinand was not called by God at all.

In our western society, when people retire, they naturally lose their title, step back from their profession, or cease labour: they retire or are removed from work and employment. Being called by God and still under their ordination vows, it is impossible for priests to "retire" from being a priest. Therefore, still called by God to serve, they are potentially available for "work". Naturally, whether they wish to continue to answer a particular call is for the individual to decide, just as they have always done. We may "retire" from a position in ministry, cease working in a particular position, or leave an appointment or office, but we do not leave or escape from our calling.

So my thoughts have turned to the difficult task of searching for a new expression for priests in these circumstances. To retire may be to withdraw, find solitude and privacy, to retreat. It can also mean to return to a place we were before, perhaps to return to the initial enthusiasm when first ordained. Retirement is when we may be able to face a new beginning of challenge, excitement, and purpose, acknowledging that there will probably exist a lower level of energy. My effort to find an acceptable new word for this time in ministry has proved challenging, but I trust the point has been noted. I need a word that singularly includes relax, replenish, reopen, and remodel. The problem is that when I enthusiastically pursue such concepts I have to lie down and rest. So until the day dawns when more acceptable terminology may be found, the word "retirement" will have to suffice.

WHAT DOES A PRIEST RELINQUISH?

Acknowledging a priest does not retire but retreats from full-time ministry can provide an altogether different aspect on what may happen when leaving full-time ministry. The demands change and alter with more choice, but often there is pain, bewilderment, and feelings of loss and bereavement. Losing position and status, local relationships, home, and some financial income can all contribute to melancholy and depression. Few other professions relinquish so much at retirement. After a lifetime of coerced busy-ness, parochial demands, and coping with parishioners' whims, an existence of possible emptiness and life in an unknown wilderness can appear threatening and overwhelming. A desire to hibernate into seclusion and obscurity can seem understandable, and this, coupled with anger at those in authority, may appear perfectly natural. But it is not the end.

After thirty-five years being fully occupied in parochial ministry and feeling under much pressure, I initially looked forward to the prospect of being free from too many conflicting demands on my time and energy. A deep-seated tiredness and a feeling of loss of direction began to pervade my ministry, even though I still enjoyed leading worship, preaching, and caring for the sick and bereaved. Working with people has brought me much joy and provided personal feelings of value when contributing to their happiness. But the responsibility of running a parish began to weigh rather heavily on my drooping shoulders.

Preparations to leave our final parish, to settle down into a different life, became more and more important as the months before the big day passed. Initially the waiting was frustrating, affected by a lifetime of working, with all the demands and pressures that working for both Church and charity meant. My wife and I did attend a local day seminar arranged by the Pensions Board, mainly on finance and housing, plus a small presentation by a tax expert. Beyond this we had hardly prepared for the future beyond the occasional comment that we should do something. After all is said and done, there is a lot more said than done. Upon reflection it would have helped if we had discussed what our plans, hopes, and expectations were with each other.

Eighteen months before the potential day of retirement my wife and I began to think about where and in what form a future home might be. Together we spent many hours looking at properties locally (which itself can be exciting but demanding) to enable us to keep in touch with children, family, and friends. We had been able to save a small amount in our accounts over the years and with the assistance of the Pensions Board we were able to purchase our present home, a bungalow, before leaving our last parish. There have been mixed reports regarding the efficiency and service of the Pensions Board, but we found them most helpful, polite, and efficiently resourceful in completing the purchase of our home.

The thought of leaving our home and ministry was difficult and admittedly a challenge. We had lived in our last parish longer than anywhere else during our then forty-three-year-long marriage. The rectory had evolved into our real home where we had put down some deep roots and enjoyed friendships with parishioners, many of them close and dear. The thought of so many "goodbyes" and tearful farewells was not something we faced enthusiastically. There were the necessary parties, acknowledgements of our ministry, and planned services which we found demanding. Naturally there were many tears, especially on our part. We experienced bereavement without a body.

WHAT DOES A PRIEST EXPERIENCE?

We were able to stay in the rectory for a little over two months after the date of retirement, which reduced the urgency of moving before the building work in our new home was completed. The gentle move went well with much help from friends and parishioners. Eventually we began to settle into our new home when a sort of "numbness" crept in, a feeling of "not-belonging" anywhere; a hazy "remoteness" overtook us as we both faced an uncertain future. It became a wilderness experience, visibly revealed in tears the following Easter Day in a different church amidst strangers. Almost unconsciously we settled into a strange non-routine, a limbo existence, feeling guilty just reading the newspaper from cover to cover before midmorning coffee. There were tensions between the two of us, with sharp words, arguments, and unacknowledged tiredness as we grappled with our new way of life. We hid from each other in keeping busy, often immersed in our personal little worlds of tasks, jobs, and making our new place a home without knowing what we really wanted. We talked to each other without real communication.

Ironically, my wife's experience of arranging and delivering relationship-skills courses to couples preparing for marriage didn't help us. Of course, we understood what was happening as we journeyed through the bereavement of losing employment, house, and home, and through finding ourselves living with a different world around us, but wisdom often disappears when uncertainty and new surroundings affect equilibrium. Even though new neighbours and acquaintances were very friendly and helpful, I remember feeling tired most of the time with little energy and enthusiasm for anything, including the things of God.

There was a humorous event in this demanding period in our conversion to a new existence. While attending a doctor's appointment with my wife, she casually mentioned to her medic about my memory. Immediately the doctor took notice, made copious notes, and arranged for an appointment with the "memory nurse". A subsequent two-hour consultation with far too many tiring questions meant a number of boxes remained unchecked, and I was referred to a memory psychiatrist in Truro. He forgot to turn up. He did, however, call to see me later in the day with many apologies. A few months later a surprise call at our home by another memory nurse revealed they had forgotten to send a letter. As you may have noted, I remember this event most clearly. Fortunately, the outcome revealed that all these problems of memory were due to overtiredness and an inability to communicate properly. We were reminded that coping with a drastic change in lifestyle, living in a new, uncertain environment, and continuing with feelings of bereavement could bring unacknowledged problems and unforeseen difficulties. But we were consciously trying to determine a new purpose and direction in life.

Advice from many people, that retirement is something to look forward to, was sadly not bearing the fruit we expected, for few mentioned the demands that twilight years might bring. One wise farmer years before had warned me with great insight that "old age ain't for cissies". Before this I had always assumed that one's body knew what it was doing, but registering with a new local surgery meant numerous tests before the medical staff would consider taking on such a risk. Now annual tests and ordered regular examinations often reveal borderline results leading to more tests and trips to hospital. These take valuable time and expense out of what I had considered leisure time. Other matters also take time, money, and energy, such as ongoing minor repairs and improvements to our new home, when previously we had been able to telephone some lovely Christian person at Diocesan Office to sort out a leaking tap, expensive tree surgery, or blocked gutters. Other expenses have to be managed, such as the Council Tax and water charges which also make inroads into our pensions. In continuing my ministry now, there are other financial demands previously claimed under parish expenses.

WHAT IS MINISTRY AFTER RETIREMENT?

After retiring I found the six-month period before being licensed with permission to officiate invaluable. Some clergy upon retiring wish to continue their ministry immediately, although in a new place and situation. I believe there are good reasons why a period of waiting is essential. For example, in continuing a ministry immediately there is the danger when leading worship and preaching in a different place that priests may forget that the congregation is no longer in their care. It is so easy to become unintentionally involved in complicating a local situation or set of circumstances. True, this can happen at any time in ministry but at retirement, by leaving one's home and community and settling into another, a priest may not be sufficiently observant or sensitive to local needs. Also, time and effort spent on solely adjusting to a new domestic situation, building firm foundations in the home, is crucial for the future whether married or single. Waiting on the Lord is a good Christian principle and allows anyone the freedom and opportunity to rediscover new things about themselves and God. Incidentally, the initials PTO for permission to officiate generally mean please turn over—a good analogy for thinking about a change in ministry and life.

In 2014, the Bishop of Truro invited me to be the retirement officer for our diocese, covering geographically almost the last western parts of the fading British Empire. The title "officer" implied to me someone who held a position of authority over subordinates, involving much bureaucracy. Throughout my long ministry I have endeavoured to be of service as taught by our Church when a deacon and following the example of our Lord Jesus. After consultation, my title has been changed to retirement chaplain: an improvement, but not settling my unease at the term "retirement". That title change will have to wait a little longer.

Currently in the Diocese of Truro there are seventy-five priests, including stipendiary, part-time, and house-for-duty, and 275 retired priests and widows and widowers in my care. A large number of priests continue their ministry by assisting and leading worship, officiating at occasional offices, teaching or leading courses, and helping in spiritual direction. Some find they are able to serve on committees and groups offering their experience and life-acquired wisdom. Without them and their contribution, God's world would be so much poorer. In the Church of England most clergy have enjoyed the freedom to move into or away from a diocese and may continue to do so during their retirement. However, it is important for those who may be able to offer the help and support available when needed to be aware of their existence. With a team of deanery chaplains and a group of trustees administering a small charitable trust in our diocese we endeavour to care for, support, and love those clergy and their partners in this corner of God's kingdom. Our diocesan bishop and staff are aware of the important contribution that retired clergy make to the life of the Church and are ensuring that all are cared for, given the parameters and resources available. Some retired clergy understandably wish to remain quietly anonymous and continue their life unconnected with ministry or with churches.

Although the first years of our retirement have passed rapidly, the experience has become joyful and positive. Home projects in house and garden, more time with our children and grandchildren, and lots of travelling and seeing friends enable us to live a life that is full. We are enjoying the relaxation and the freedom to choose what we wish to do. Now visitors call just for social reasons, we enjoy answering the telephone, are able to contribute to our community in a different way, and slowly our new home is becoming a real home. True, in our twilight years we are aware of the lower levels of energy, the need to take more time caring for each other, and the more frequent health issues that can occur. But there is more choice: not the "god of choice" such as offered by politicians in health and services, but real choice given natural limitations to continue in ministry. This has continued at a slower and less demanding pace with time to prepare more thoughtfully for worship in and around our part of God's world. We have both been made most welcome wherever my ministry has led. There has been more time available to reflect and consider what I really wish for and what God may wish for me.

Reflecting on my past parochial ministry, it often felt I was subjugating myself in the cause of a Church making too many demands in keeping the institution going rather than helping others find God and themselves. That might have been necessary in the eyes of God, who no doubt has long-term plans for God's people and has to prepare for the future. Now within a new ministry I am beginning to find myself again—to offer something different and more reflective to the People of God whom I try to serve. Some clergy are quite happy being responsible for buildings, finance, and maintenance, but I, being more gregarious and people-orientated, always found these matters difficult, in spite of re-roofing, repairing, and upgrading two medieval churches to the tune of over half a million pounds.

There is now evolving a new life of Christ's love in which I feel more confident. I can now choose to explore and learn with others more about the kingdom of heaven, and find time for theological reflection which gives me confidence in sharing my experience of the love of God, without the burdens of administration and local politics. I can lead worship, preach, and share the Word with new, refreshing insight and with the added benefits of time to reflect on past ministry. But as has been the case for so many Christians, this has come with a journey through a wilderness, just as it was for Jesus and his disciples who often hardly knew where they were to spend the next night. Death and resurrection is not a once-only personal event, but a daily experience as we are transformed into the life of eternal love.

In spite of age and dwindling energy, God continues to call, opening up a whole new world of service to the People of God. As the years roll on and the twilight years race by, there is always something that can be done and offered, for even the least mobile can pray for the Church's ministry in sharing the wonderful world of the gospel. The over-busy, frightening, and demanding world is in great need of priests with time, patience, and theological reflection to bring their gifts to bear. So in many new and exciting ways those no longer employed in full-time ministry can escape retirement and find their true selves again.

3. RETIREMENT OR BEREAVEMENT?

Katy Morgan

Many people really look forward to the day when they can finish work and do whatever they want to do each day. However, for some, retirement does not come easily, and I am one of those people. In fact, I found it very difficult. To understand my feelings about retirement, you need to know a bit about me and my ministry, so here we go.

My first three years of ordained ministry were as an MSE (Minister in Secular Employment), or as it was called then, NSM (Non-Stipendiary Minister). I had been a primary school teacher for twenty-five years, and was then teaching part-time, living just outside the city. I served as curate for three years in a nice suburban parish across on the other side. Then the bishop allowed me to transfer to stipendiary ministry. He wisely insisted that full-time ministry would be different and that I should serve another curacy, so I was side-stepped into a neighbouring, but very different, city parish.

Socially, this was a challenging area, with some old city families, a new estate development, and quite a few families who were rehoused into council homes when, years ago, the docks were redeveloped. I loved it. I had actually lived there before, as my father was vicar there for five years. In fact, I believe I made history as the first woman priest to serve in the parish in which her father had served before her. It made the local television news and the national papers, including a line in *The Times*, and even a paragraph in an American paper. No one has disputed the claim yet. I was quite resentful of having to serve another curacy, but the bishop was quite right, and it certainly prepared me for the next step.

INCUMBENCY

Two years later a friend and colleague who was about to leave her incumbency encouraged me to apply for her job. I did so and was appointed. So began twelve years of happy, busy, and fulfilling ministry. Of course, it had its moments, but again, I loved it.

The parish was in a large "village" which had grown extensively over the years, and was almost joined on to the city but not quite. It had only one church, built in 1957, with a Garden of Remembrance, but no graveyard and no peal of bells . . . cushy? Actually, no. There were around 12,000 people, again with a mixture of social challenges. The old village up the road and beyond the railway line had its own church and vicar, and many of the 6,000 people who lived there were in professional or managerial employment, or retirement. Our estate, at the lower end of the village, had been built for the workers of a local factory and consisted mainly of pleasant semi-detached houses, owned by their inhabitants.

A main road ran through my parish and really divided it. On the other side of this road there was another small estate of what were previously council houses, now run by a housing association. Many of these homes housed single-parent families and folk coping with financial hardship and/or drug problems. Just down the road from this small estate was an MOD Air Force base, with all of its housing "outside the wire", as they call it—in other words not enclosed within the camp boundaries. This was sandwiched between the small estate and another quite large council estate. So taken as a whole, this was very much a "tiered" village, divided by the railway line, the main road, and the RAF station.

Although there were many families with young children living here, our congregation was made up of mainly older couples, widows, and widowers, for whom we catered very well. We did not seem to be doing the right things to attract younger people, unlike the charismatic evangelical church up the road. So the village benefitted from two different traditions and people could choose the church which nourished and nurtured them best. There was also a Methodist church and a Roman Catholic church in the village, and we worked as Churches Together on several occasions during the year.

We had an excellent resource with our simple, light church, a large hall with a stage, a smaller meeting room, a good kitchen, and lots of parking. The hall was really well used by the church, the community, and the diocese. Every day there was a different group, ranging from our TOTS group and Brownies to Slimming World, from the local drama group to a twice-monthly meal for the elderly. It was really important to me that I should regularly visit these groups, which obviously took time and energy.

We were a eucharistic worshipping community. Each day began and ended with the daily office in church, there was a midweek Eucharist, and three services on a Sunday, with the addition of noon baptisms twice a month. During my twelve years there I trained four curates, helped another finish her curacy after a difficult time elsewhere, and encouraged several trainees or explorers on placement with me. Over several years a group of us trained as a local ministry team, which enabled and encouraged many of the congregation to discover different ministries within the life of the church and in the wider community.

For five years I was also officiating chaplain at the local RAF camp, and this was an enjoyable experience. As well as presiding over Christmas, Harvest, and other occasional services, I was privileged to be involved with supporting the families of those serving in Iraq during the war in Iraq, along with helping service men and women with problems. Then the RAF moved elsewhere.

All this went on alongside the day-to-day routine of administration, of the usual pastoral work of visiting people in their homes and in hospital, of funerals (quite a few) and weddings (not many)—all the things a parish priest does. I was fortunate in that my husband took early retirement from his managerial role as a chartered accountant and became a house husband, so I was relieved of much on the home front. However, after ten years of working at this intensive pace, and heading towards my sixtieth birthday, I was beginning to get tired.

RETIREMENT?

Five years before, my husband and I had gone on a day of preparation
for retirement held by the diocese. It covered housing options, savings,
pensions, and so on; actually nothing which really helped us personally.
We were fortunate enough to own a property, and with my husband's
background we were sorted. There was a session on the emotional side
of retirement, but it was so far in advance that it made little impact at
that time.

I had thought I was to retire at the age of sixty, and mentally I was
preparing myself for this. Then the Government declared a change in
pensionable age, and my pensionable date was moved to age sixty-two
and a half. This was quite a blow, and it took me a long while to adjust
to the idea. In fact, I don't think I really did at all. It meant that I had to
keep going, as we couldn't manage financially without my state pension,
so I soldiered on. At the age of sixty-one, just before Christmas, I almost
cracked. I was utterly exhausted. I was told by the diocese that I could
either go to the doctor and get signed off (just before Christmas) or grit
my teeth and carry on, taking some time off in the new year. I don't give
in very easily, so I carried on.

Then, in the January, God sent me a lifeboat. A dear elderly friend died
and left me some money, which enabled me to announce my retirement.
We decided on the beginning of September, as I had two weddings
already planned which I wanted to honour. So began the approach to
the big move and change of life.

The property we owned was not suitable for us to live in permanently,
so we started to look for another house. We eventually found one we
could afford, so much smaller than we were used to, in a town not too
far away, and where our daughter, her husband, and their two children
live. Over the next few months my husband spent a lot of time there
decorating and getting it ready for us.

This actually proved to be a problem for me. Of course, it should not
have been, I know, and I should have only been grateful for all the effort
he put in . . . and he did a wonderful job. However, I was so busy back
in the parish that I was not able to spend much time with him, helping
him, so, although he always included me in decisions made, I came to feel

that the house was his, not mine. Childish? Maybe, but real. There was perhaps also resentment that I had to carry on working while he could spend time in our future home. I do not really know how we could have handled it differently, but I flag it up as a danger area to be thought about and avoided if possible for about-to-retire clergy in a similar position.

I am a sentimental person and a natural hoarder, so with six months to go we started to think about clearing out the loft, the garage, and the spare room. What a nightmare. As time went on we became more concerned about finishing it all on time. I found it to be a very painful exercise, having to get rid of so much of our past. I had kept lots of things from our children's past as well as my own, and it was a wrench to let it go, but I had to. There was just no space in the new house.

I cannot bear to bin things which might be of use to someone, so the local charity shops did very well. We ended up, in desperation, piling things at the end of our drive for anyone to take away. People thought this was great, especially the children, and were thrilled to take away a freebie or six. The walk to and from school became quite exciting for them that week.

The parish gave me the most wonderful send-off, with a really moving service of farewell and a terrific party. It was a sad day, having to say goodbye to the people with whom I had lived so closely for twelve years. I knew it was my decision, and I knew it had to happen, but it was still incredibly difficult. Having walked with them through good times and bad, sharing their joy and their grief, encouraging them and watching them grow and flourish in their faith and in their individual ministries, it was hard to let them go, but I had to, so I did. The move happened, with grateful thanks to two of my sisters who were able to come over to help sort and clean. I hated everything about that day. I am sure I should have felt excited, but I did not. I simply felt bereft. So retirement began.

THE FIRST FEW MONTHS

The first week or two was just like being on holiday, and we did have some time away in France, so that was not too bad. However, as time went on it began to dawn on me that this was how it was going to be from now on.

I wandered aimlessly through the days, waking each morning thinking, "What can I do today?" and feeling an emptiness that overwhelmed me. I missed my ministry, and did not feel useful or needed any more, though I know that was ridiculous. I hated living in "our" house, and missed having my own space, my study, to retreat to. For me, retirement was a four-fold bereavement. I had lost: my job, for which I had been called and trained; my daily contact with all the people I had been working with, sharing with and loving; my home; and much of my past.

Bereavement often follows a pattern, including sadness, disbelief, anger, resentment, and apathy in varying degrees. This was true of my existence for the next few months. In my tiredness and confusion, I was even having real doubts about my faith, which was very scary. The first Sunday after our short holiday, we went to the Eucharist at the church in which we had decided to worship. I cried the whole way through. Other people were up front, doing what I had been doing for so many years, which was so much a part of me and my ministry, and which I would probably never do regularly again. The next week I only cried for half the service, and as the weeks went by I got more used to it. The vicar was very understanding, and his sympathy helped.

Having said all these negative things, on the positive side it was indeed a relief not to have the pressures of incumbency. I no longer had to worry about the toilets being blocked, or the roof leaking. I did not have to sort out the dispute between two people, or placate someone who had had their flowers stolen from the Garden of Remembrance. I missed the interaction with the people, I missed saying the daily office with others, I really missed taking services, especially the Eucharist, and I even missed writing sermons, but this space enabled my exhausted body, mind, and spirit to rest. It *had* to be, and though it was probably the most difficult time in my life so far, looking back on it, it *was* a healing time.

I struggled through the months till Christmas. All the advice given to me was "Do not take anything on for at least six months", but I was just not coping with the emptiness. So I decided it was time to do something to help myself. On my first appointment with our new doctor I was officially classed as "obese" (actually, that is not as bad as it sounds) and was offered twelve free sessions with Slimming World on the NHS. So I went, and tried reasonably hard not to eat the wrong things, and to add a regular walk to the exercise routine given to me by the osteopath for my painful hip. In a year I lost a stone and a half, which made me feel better about myself. I would like to lose a little bit more, so that is one of my aims for the future.

I joined the University of the Third Age (U3A) and signed up for a beginners' art class. I have always loved drawing, especially portraits, but had never been taught the skills needed to make the portraits "real", and my paintings were very childish. It was the best thing I could have done. So every Friday morning I went along and spent two hours doing something I really enjoyed, something that was for me. I had not really done much for me while I was working. This class has been one of the highlights of my retirement. Not only have I learnt many skills, but I have also been part of a community of lovely people who have taken me for who I am, and not expected great things from me. I still love it today.

I continue to sing in a local choir, which, as a trained singer, has always been a joy. We rehearse once a week and give four concerts a year, two comprising oratorio works and two lighter programmes.

Another thing I did for "me" was swimming. I have always loved to swim, and as part of their incredibly generous leaving present, my congregation gave me an eighteen-month subscription to the local swimming pool. Again, I have become part of a community of like-minded people, as it tends to be the same people who swim regularly. We even stay behind on certain days for coffee together, and last month we had a meal out together.

Just before Christmas I was asked to consider taking on the chaplaincy of a local Sea Cadet unit, which I agreed to do. This entails going several times a month to chat with the cadets and the staff, be there for any who want to talk through a personal issue, teach the cadets about the Core Values (honesty and integrity, commitment, self discipline, loyalty and respect), prepare them for enrolment, and say prayers at Divisions (parade) once a month.

I have always had a strong connection with our local cathedral, so another thing I offered was to be chaplain to the visitors one morning a month. It is wonderful to spend time in that beautiful holy space and be available for those who come looking for help, or are there as tourists experiencing the awe, the majesty, and the peace of God's house. I take a midweek Eucharist there now and again, too.

All of these things have been invaluable in settling me more into retirement. Maybe I took on too much too soon, which went against all the advice I was given, but I think for me, it was important to keep busy.

INTERIM DUTY

The next thing which really helped was a request several months later from the archdeacon to help out in a nearby benefice with two churches during their vacancy. I was missing parish ministry a great deal, so this was another lifeboat. I offered two Sundays a month, plus occasional offices. In the three months, May to July, I took ten weddings, which of course included all the preparation meetings and rehearsals, a few funerals and umpteen baptisms, as well as their Sunday morning Eucharists. It was a most fulfilling time, and it was just what I needed to help me through this stage of "ministry nothingness". It was busy, but not "full-on", and I could say "no" if necessary. By the time the new incumbent was licensed I had worked through much of my bereavement, and was on the way to realizing the peace which retirement could bring.

Over these months I became known by the local undertakers and was asked to take several funerals. Funeral ministry is one of my strengths, so this has been a wonderful opportunity for me to carry out my ministry in a fulfilling and privileged way. This has built up through time, and I now often have to say no.

One unfortunate incident, which I am sure has happened to many other priests after retirement, was a misunderstanding between me and the new incumbent of my former parish. I was asked to take the funeral of a parishioner with whom I had had many dealings. As far as I was concerned I observed the correct protocol, sending them straight to the incumbent, but what they actually said to her I do not know, because the next day I had a gentle reprimand from the diocesan officer for retired clergy in my deanery. Evidently the incumbent was very upset and felt I should not be involved as she was now vicar. This really upset me, as I have a strong sense of injustice, and I felt a reprimand was uncalled for. I had done everything by the book. It *was* her first incumbency, I *had* been there for twelve years and was well loved, so perhaps it was understandable. It was sorted out eventually, but has left its mark. So I flag this up as a warning. On retirement you will have people asking you to do things for them. As much as you love them, be careful. I understand and agree that you must keep away and allow the new person to establish themselves, but even after the statutory year had gone by, I found it very difficult feeling that I had to creep into the parish to visit those special friends who cannot get out to visit me. It is a really difficult situation, and one to be prepared for.

As we live very close to the diocesan border, I applied for permission to officiate in the next diocese. The nearest benefice to our town had recently gone into a vacancy, and with many churches to cover they have over time sought my help. This means that I get to preside at the Eucharist, as and when I am able and want to, so fulfilling that precious priestly role which is so much a part of me and which I was missing so much. I have also been invited to take two half-hour slots in their Good Friday three-hour service. This has involved research and preparation, and I have thoroughly enjoyed the opportunity.

In my past I have helped to run sessions and weekends on Local Ministry Team training courses. A year after my retirement date I was invited to co-facilitate, voluntarily, on the Diocesan Pastoral Assistant course, which has developed from the LMT ethos. We are now on our third course and I am really enjoying it, although of course I'm still learning. We cover topics such as pastoral visiting, bereavement visiting, marriage and baptism preparation, confidentiality, boundaries, and so on; in each of these areas I have much experience to offer, together with my years of teaching experience. In this role I feel I am using my teaching, my ministry, and my skills to good advantage, and helping the diocese in the process.

RELAXING INTO RETIREMENT

Eighteen months down the line I am gradually relaxing into retirement. Yes, it's really taken this long. The services I am called in for are now enough, and I am getting quite good at saying no. I am enjoying my art, my swimming, my music, and especially my family. Our daughter pops in regularly with our two grandsons, and we love having the time to spend with them. Watching them grow and develop is a real joy. It is also good to have so much more free time to babysit, and to be available for the school pick-up time. I know our daughter appreciates that too.

If the weather is nice, or we want something from Ikea, we can just go out for the day, so time I can now spend with my husband is a bonus. We can go off on short holidays when we want to, and can even go away for weekends. No longer are we tied by Sundays. Every now and again I meet my old friends over here, in a local tea shop. I am even slowly accepting living in *our* house, and we have plans to extend, building on another room for me and all my art-and-craft stuff: my own space. I am also thinking through what I really want to keep on doing, and what I want now to let go; I am getting more selective.

I vaguely remember someone a long time ago saying to me, "Do not underestimate retirement." This is now my mantra for anyone who enjoys their job as much as I loved my ministry. It *may* be wonderful for you, but it *can* truly be a great bereavement, which needs time to work through. Talking to other retired clergy, I am not alone in this deep sense of loss which I have experienced. Several also felt that they have a great deal of expertise to offer which the diocese could use.

I have just had a conversation with our new bishop about some better preparation for those about to retire, particularly on the emotional side, and about maybe giving retired clergy the opportunities to use their gifts and experience to help others, as I am doing with the pastoral assistant course. Hopefully the diocese will think about these things and action them.

Looking to the future, I can see ahead a gentler pace of life, with time to think, to feel, to read, and to pray. The incredible pressures of full-time ministry are behind me, and I can let them go, yet I can still have a ministry. I am more hopeful and more at peace. Retirement is finally arriving, and it looks as though it could be good after all.

4. VOCATION VERSUS RETIREMENT

Judy Howard

Sitting in the summer house in our garden I reflect on retirement; what it felt like, what it continues to feel like, what it means, for me and for others who share this transition in its many guises. Being invited to write about the experience of retiring as a clergy person in the Church of England evokes a mixture of responses.

For clergy who are parish priests, retirement requires a letting go of job, home, church community, neighbours, and wider community. The severing is total. The etiquette is that the retired priest does not go back to the parish for a significant space of time. I have watched this totality of leaving in members of our family who have lived and taught in a boarding school environment all their working life. There is total commitment to one piece of geography and its people. I wonder in what other walks of life does retirement bring such complete change. Who am I? What am I for? Where am I going? Where do I belong?

I was ordained into a self-supporting ministry, so remained in my home and commuted eleven miles to the parish in which I served for nine years, first as curate and then as associate priest. I was never the vicar of a parish, living in a vicarage. For me, home remained the same. Involvement in my village community was exchanged for immersion in diverse inner-city communities; traditional rural parish church for multi-everything inner-city parish church.

Ordination never completely took over my identity. When to wear and when not to wear the dog collar was a constant source of discomfort.

In many ways, I have often sensed a greater affinity with the laity than the clergy since, like them, I have always been a volunteer. Or perhaps a bridge, belonging to both laity and clergy.

The key issues for me, in retirement, have not been to do with housing or finance. They are issues which are equally relevant to anyone retiring or going through major change: issues of bereavement, identity, value, and place in the community. There are the positive issues for retired clergy like the freedom which allows a more prophetic place in the Church; freedom from dreary "club" meetings; freedom to belong to a wider Christian family than a particular parish; freedom to explore and voice a more radical theology; and freedom and time to belong to the wider world.

EXPERIENCING BEREAVEMENT

Thinking of retirement, my mind goes back to my last day in the parish, Easter Sunday, all glory and outpouring of kindness. And then that walking away, amidst a sea of goodbyes, from nine years of belonging to a people and a place. Then a few weeks later and the first Sunday of my new dispensation, walking tentatively to church, creeping in, wanting not to be noticed, not ready to belong. Bereavement needs time.

That Sunday when I walked back into the church, in the village in which I live, despite having belonged for years before ordination, I no longer knew my shape or role, where or how my piece of life fitted in. I now sat through services I wanted to alter, sang hymns I would never have chosen, yearned for a more diverse community, and imagined how I would reorder everything. When invited to go onto the coffee rota I winced.

All that embarrassing reaction from having been important, used to being at the front, leading, having power, making the choices, and now starting to earn my belonging from the bottom up. What a terrible hierarchical image, but it is often the way things are in church. Before ordination I had been a reader for eight years in my village church, and led non-Eucharistic worship, preached, robed, and took funerals. Now I did not have a licence to do any of those things. Permission to officiate

(PTO) takes months to process, and the policy of our diocese is not to grant it for a year after retirement.

Neither was I a straightforward lay person again. I wondered whether I could visit the sick as a friend or whether that would be regarded as touting for potential funeral custom, stepping into the vicar's territory. How did the wider community beyond church now view me? To many people anyone who wears a dog collar, however occasionally, is a "vicar". How would the new—to me—vicar view me? Would I be a threat? Could I be a resource? Did I want to be? What was my vocation now? I wanted to hide.

Fortunately, that summer, I had an accident which made me immobile for some weeks. That gave me permission to opt out, to spend time just sitting in the garden, waiting, and being, reading, and thinking, wondering how long it takes for the ache of missing to ease.

NEW BEGINNINGS

Six years on from that retirement Easter Sunday, and another vicar on from the day I walked back into my village church, I am preparing to take a baptism tomorrow morning; I led a retreat day for fifteen ordinands last Wednesday; took a funeral last Saturday; will be leading a Lent group next Tuesday; sat in our summer house this morning listening to someone who comes for spiritual direction; and sat with the benefice staff team yesterday afternoon in the vicarage. All this is woven through family life, with nine grandchildren, and a mother next door who is nearly ninety-six years old.

The life-long seeking of vocation runs deeper than any particular stage or role or label. As I moved through those early months of "retirement", I started to attend to these deeper seams of identity, the undercurrent of calling. It is like exploring through the annual rings of a tree, in and in through the layers, each strengthening and supporting the next year's growth.

I was licensed as a reader in 1993. This gave accreditation to a busy lay ministry of children's work, family services, leading study and prayer groups, and all the things that members of church communities become involved in—Church Council, fundraising, taking part in weekly worship, and being on the coffee and washing up rota. All this was the church club stuff: what about beneath and beyond that?

We lived in, and still live in, a house with enough space to accommodate groups of all ages. It has been the perfect place to bring up a family, to fill with children and friends and relations. My husband, a passionate gardener, has created a beautiful garden which we open for charity and share with many people. We belong to tribal families who love big gatherings and have many friends to visit. So a natural ministry of hospitality had grown up here over the years.

Shortly after being licensed as a reader I was introduced to The Quiet Garden Trust. We joined and started to offer regular Quiet Days here, using the house and the garden. This ministry grew to include spiritual direction, and space for individuals to have retreat time. Then other groups started to come, secular and church groups.

The vision of the Quiet Garden Trust is to initiate and resource a network of local opportunities for silence, solitude, and the appreciation of beauty; for the teaching of contemplative prayer; and for the experience of creativity and healing in the context of God's love. People have spoken of these experiences having spent time here.

Through the commuting years, away from the village and working several days a week in the inner-city parish, this home ministry continued. And then it was added to by a bus load of inner-city parishioners coming for summer picnics, and clergy teams coming for away days to work together in a peaceful space. So when "retirement" from my particular parish and church community happened, and after the initial bereavement eased a little, I was able to listen to these other layers of vocation afresh.

An image emerged for me. The design of the central part of our garden is like the foundations of a great Benedictine abbey. My husband had been unaware of this pattern in his design, but maybe the structural forms of our cultural heritage lie more deeply within our psyche than we realize. The edges of the garden are informal, leading into the wild. Perhaps these areas reflect a more Celtic spirituality. So our garden, in some quiet, unselfconscious way, seemed to become a "monastic" space for a fluid community.

Another model that emerged for me was that of the Beguinage. These houses of lay communities of women, committed to prayer on behalf of their towns and villages, emerged in the Low Countries. I understand that women could become Beguines for flexible periods of time, unlike a monastic commitment. You could come apart from the normal routine of life and commit yourself to prayer for a period and then return to the duties of family and work. So the people who come apart for a Quiet Day share in this rhythm. In "retirement", I had more time to attend to this vocation of a monastic hospitality, a playful rather than heavily pious concept, and it has continued to call me on a journey of exploration.

One of the aspects of bereavement, in the early days, was the loss of the daily opportunity for God talk, that is, meaningful theological reflection and nourishment with colleagues and parishioners. When you are a professional theologian you are expected to talk "God". I realized that no one was going to provide this for me and that I needed to take responsibility to read, to find like-minded people with whom to meet and purposefully talk theology, and to find opportunities for learning.

At that time, when I enquired, I was told that continuing clergy training was for the non-retired. I was fortunate to have friends, both retired and non-retired, who were keen for a theology group. We met in one another's homes and took it in turns to bring an issue, an insight, a question. I also have a sister who runs a Christian bookshop, and she supplies me with current reading and stimulating conversation. As I write, the most recent diocesan bulletin for retired clergy is encouraging us to attend a variety of further learning opportunities, for which I am most grateful.

The Quiet Garden days here have provided a fertile ground for theological exploration with the informal community of people who attend. The safe space has allowed for courageous vulnerability, for voicing what might be unspeakable in most church gatherings, and to let go and rediscover at a profound and life-giving level. It also attracts people from diverse Christian backgrounds and some who do not profess religious affiliation.

I valued greatly and missed deeply, when I retired, the professional sphere, the space in which I was known and related to as a professional woman. At home and in the village community I assumed that I was primarily known as a wife, a mother, a daughter, and a grandmother. All those are intrinsic parts of my identity. But there is an independence and strength in being able to operate as a professional. That professional awareness, that I thought I had lost, has come back and more deeply over the years. I just need to be aware of it and to own it. Rather than consciously picking it up, it seems to clothe me in situations where it is needed; I think it flows from a vocation of presence.

PRECARIOUS NEW IDENTITY

It is interesting how a title allows dignity. To be Reverend was natural, normal, during life in the parish. Since retirement I am addressed, on envelopes, in a variety of ways: Judy Howard; Mrs J. M. Howard; the Revd J. Howard; Mrs Philip Howard; and we even received a Christmas card addressed to Mr and Rev. Philip Howard.

On one occasion, when invited to a very smart dinner party, we were sent a list of attendees beforehand. Beside the man's name, in each couple, a synopsis of his professional life was given. The women had nothing written about them. They were all given their husbands' names. One woman was a widow. Beside her name were the professional achievements of her dead husband; nothing about her considerable achievements.

In retirement, I do not want to wander around in a dog collar. Some do. And when I put one on, I do feel different, sometimes conspicuous, and I am treated differently. Sometimes that disturbs me, sets me apart, closes conversation down. Sometimes it is a gift, allowing for a depth of conversation and trust that might not otherwise occur. I hope that my true dignity, my identity, can primarily be as a human being.

I remember Bishop John Taylor, formerly Bishop of Winchester, telling me that after retirement he realized that during his working life his diary had told him who he was. Without it he was not sure who he was any longer. He also told me of an experience he had waiting at a bus stop, being an "ordinary" person, and seeing himself in his past life as a monkey on a chain, dancing to the crowd. This image has stayed with me and I realize how important it is to find identity beneath the roles and the robes and the titles.

How easy to lose our primary value as human, and how wonderful to be absorbed anonymously into the crowd and to belong to the crowd. That is what I love about sitting on a London bus. But I realize that for many this anonymity is a loneliness I never have to experience.

Within a year of my retirement, the vicar of my village parish was off work with periods of illness and I was asked to step in and be involved with the leading of services in the benefice. I was also asked to take funerals and weddings. I attended the local ministry team meetings, and, together with the associate priest, another retired priest, and a reader, worked with the churchwardens to cover services in the benefice, to lead groups, and to provide pastoral care. I was clear that my vocation was primarily local, that I did not feel called to fill gaps on rotas further afield. If our garden and home were my "monastery", local was my commitment to the stability of monastic rule.

However, when this vicar retired, and we entered a period of vacancy, the diocese, with no apparent conversation with any of the existing ministry team, imposed an interim minister. I assume that it was thought to be a supportive move. The churchwardens were given virtually no notice. I returned from holiday to find a stranger, who was not resident in the parish, running everything, and with no reference to the ministry team. It felt deeply disrespectful to all of us who comprised the local church, as though we could not exist as "Church" without an imported dog collar. I had worked with the Local Ministry Scheme in our diocese for seven years, from its inception, and have always been passionate about lay and ordained members of the church working together in collaborative ministry. What we had built up and practised seemed to us to be totally disregarded by the central authority of the Church.

While all this was happening, despite having permission to officiate from the bishop, my name and details continued to be left off the diocesan register. I know this was an administrative error, but it seemed to accentuate the experience of being erased from the consciousness of the diocese once I had "retired".

Another administrative "error", regarding retired clergy, was when the painful rejection of the vote to consecrate women as bishops came through and the pastoral letters of support for the women clergy in the diocese were only sent to currently serving clergy. As though forgotten was the fact that it was those retired women priests who had been the first to be ordained and struggled for that justice. All the flurry of emails and messages which circulated immediately never landed on my screen or that of any of us who were retired. Delayed was the comfort for our pain. We had to find our own source of solidarity through those first hours of disbelief. I was fortunate to have dear friends who were still serving as non-retired clergy. They kept me in the loop, and sane.

Something quite different which I still struggle with adjusting to is the lumping together of "retired clergy" as a category in the consciousness of the diocese. It seems a good thing that our diocese has set up caring oversight for the retirees, providing a retired clergy person in each deanery to keep an eye on those who are retired in their patch. I imagine that this is particularly welcoming for clergy who move into the diocese in retirement and have no existing networks to belong to. Social events for, and visits to each retired clergy person are offered. Once a year we are all invited to tea on the lawn of the bishop's house and spouses are included.

There was a time when clergy spouses, wives of course then, would be used to attending church events as a couple. But in today's world this cannot be an assumption. I did not want to belong to a club of retired clergy and have never felt that the category of retired clergy fitted. My husband would be horrified to be lumped into a category of clergy spouses, and he would far rather be on the golf course than having tea with a bunch of retired clergy on the bishop's lawn. This may sound ungrateful. I am simply trying to be honest about how patronizing this can somehow feel.

BEYOND RETIREMENT

If it is true that the retired clergy in the Church of England are vital to its operation and survival, in its present structure, does this simplistic division of retired and non-retired convey anything meaningful? I wonder how we might think differently about the human resource of the people who make up "church" in any particular diocese or parish. "Retirement" is not used to categorize the usefulness or otherwise of lay

Christians. Their contribution to the body of Christ has nothing to do with being retired or not.

There seems to be tragic waste in the deployment of skilled, experienced lay and retired ministers in the church. I hear sad stories from those who have much to give and feel put out to grass. The latest national directive for retired clergy reads as though we are public enemy number one for sitting incumbents.

It takes imaginative, generous clergy on the ground to find, to listen to, and to utilize the local human resource, which the church has often spent time and cost in training in the first place. It is as though, with each new incumbent, we start all over again. I am grateful to have an incumbent who has affirmed my ministry in the parish, both the church "club" ministry and the vocation that lies beyond church.

Retirement provides space to step outside the box, to be freed up from the pressures of "running the show", and of being responsible for plant and finance. Physically moving from the centre of operation to the edge gives a fresh perspective, an opportunity to do more prophetic theological reflection. It seems a time to risk some more radical thinking and action. Since I retired, I have become involved with an "alternative expression" of church. I have time now to attend their service on some Sunday mornings and have been invited to celebrate communion there each month.

Some who attend are members of parish churches, often hanging on by the skin of their teeth. For them these contemplative services are the nourishment that gives them the courage to stay "in" their parish church, and a place in which to explore theology. The majority are people who became disenfranchised with traditional church, who value exploring other faiths, and who are deeply committed to spiritual practices. From connections with people who attend these gatherings, conversations with other groups have emerged. I have been invited to share my spiritual path and then to share communion. Bread and wine have been a homecoming. These times have been profound, often accompanied by tears.

I remember, years ago, reading a definition of "the prophet". It suggested that when we find the *status quo* of a group unbearable we have the choice to stay in and shut up; to leave and speak out (but then we lose the context to which our speaking out is relevant); or to stay in and speak out. This final option is the stance of the prophet. It seems that this can be a role for those of us who are called retired. We can belong to the church but in a sufficiently non-attached sense to be able to have an edge perspective from which we have a responsibility to speak and act. There have been times when I have had to say to myself, "The worst that will happen is that I will be sacked." Somehow that seems less drastic from a retired perspective.

Despite the experiences of being "erased" from the consciousness of the diocese, there have been far more times when I have been affirmed. I have spoken to people in high places, area deans and bishops and diocesan departmental heads, and told these stories. I asked for permission to take communion to these groups I have mentioned and have received such gracious affirmation. I have been blessed, literally, for the journey.

Retirement has brought bereavement and blessing, great adjustment and new freedom, neglect and affirmation. I have been exasperated with, and hurt by, the institution of church and imagined opting out. It has also given me experiences of the greatest blessing and glory. All this will be in solidarity with countless others over the ages, both lay and ordained Christians. I have valued reflecting on my own experiences of retirement and the issues that have arisen. If I am honest, I never feel or think of myself as "retired", and my diary does not look like it either.

Sitting in the summer house again, looking across the pond and the lower part of the garden, I see my husband busy working on the changes to the garden, necessary for the building of our new smaller house. Building starts next month and will take a year. So it is all change. A very small move in terms of distance and yet a huge move in terms of the whole of our shared family life. Our son and his family will move into our present house.

It is interesting that several people have referred to this move as being our retirement.

My husband "retired" from running his landscape business twelve years ago, and I left the inner-city parish six years ago. Did we retire then? Will we retire again next year when we move down the garden, next to the hens? Do we all retire many times in different ways? I wonder. Is retirement a useful term, a meaningful term, a helpful term? I wonder what you, the reader, experience, or dread, or look forward to?

5. AN EARLY RETIREMENT?

John Eatock

When did my retirement begin? That is the question! In 1992 (aged forty-seven), I resigned my incumbency of a parish in East Lancashire in the Diocese of Blackburn. I also resigned my post as rural dean of Accrington, along with my appointments to various diocesan committees and as acting CME officer. I saw this move as part of my personal development and a continuation of my vocation as a priest. It was part of my own mid-life crisis, I guess, and I had no one urging me to make a move away from parochial ministry other than myself. Was this a response to the prompting of the Spirit, or was it my own wilfulness? It would take too much space to explore the myriad of reasons and events that led to this decision.

I had recently trained, as part of my own continuing professional development, as a counsellor/psychotherapist. During this training I had a placement in a GP surgery one day a week on my day off. The fall in prescribing of medication for mild to moderate mental health conditions was dramatic, and I found myself invited by a group of doctors in Eccles, Manchester, to be their practice counsellor. I stayed working in that GP practice in various guises until 2003, continuously developing my expertise and adding various other professional roles, such as university lecturer, consultant to a cancer support centre, representative of the local branch of the British Association for Counselling and Psychotherapy, occasional trainer of GPs at local postgraduate medical institutes, and other similar activities.

TRANSITIONING TO SELF-SUPPORTING MINISTRY

The transition to becoming what was, in fact, a self-supporting priest with a work-based focus was interesting. On leaving parochial ministry, I had a perfectly affable interview with my diocesan bishop, who assured me that I would soon be requesting a return to parochial ministry, and I was given permission to officiate (PTO). There was no question as to how I would cope with the move from a "tied house" to our own property. In fact, there was little if any exploration of the motives or the vocational implications of this decision by my diocesan bishop. The move, as it happened, was not too difficult in respect of finding somewhere to live and, with the help of our modest savings and a loan from a friend, we managed to obtain a mortgage for a small terraced house adjacent to our former parish. On the advice of our financial advisor, I moved my accumulated pension from the Church Commissioners Scheme to an investment portfolio: a move that has proved to be excellent in providing for my second "retirement".

The whole issue of whether or not we could survive outside the Church with its tied housing and other benefits was difficult, and we were told that we would never be able to live our lives at the same fiscal level as those of equivalent age: in short, that we would never "catch up". Fortunately, my wife is an excellent manager, and we have always lived within our means, even in difficult times, and we continue to do so and to maintain our charitable giving. My income has oscillated in my so-called retirement and was especially challenging during the early years of self-employment. Beginning with a mortgage alongside a large debt at the age of forty-seven is not the easiest way to begin a "retired life".

From that moment of resignation and surrender of my licences I had no official contact with the diocese other than invitations to events for retired clergy. The Church of England, certainly in my diocese at that time, made the assumption that someone who had resigned their living was, for all practical purposes, "retired". It felt exceedingly strange, since I continued to say the Office, endeavoured to keep up to date theologically and liturgically, and worshipped at a local church. It was only gradually that I began to feel that my priestly ministry was indeed fulfilled in my occupation as a counsellor/psychotherapist. Furthermore, it seemed that the outside world was very interested in my gifts, particularly in my experience of pastoral care and human relations, and my employing GPs were certainly concerned for my welfare. There was a definite feeling of "detachment" from the Church which had nurtured, trained, and employed me for more than twenty years. I never felt inclined to attend events for the "retired clergy", and I wrote to protest at being assumed to be in that category. The invitations nevertheless continued, and it seemed as though my situation was entirely misunderstood. Ordained colleagues at that time did not seem to know how to position me in the structure of the Church.

I enjoyed "going to church", observing from the pew, and working the hours that others considered to be a normal working week. From time to time, I would be invited to preside at the Eucharist or to preach, although these occasions back in the 1990s were few and far between. I was, it seemed, an anomaly, semi-detached, retired in the eyes of the hierarchy, and perhaps an embarrassment, as I had made the unusual move away from parochial ministry into secular employment.

The financial situation in working as a self-employed primary care counsellor/psychotherapist in the uncertain world of the NHS for a group of innovative doctors in a downtown medical centre was, at times, precarious. Like many self-employed people, I began to take up any opportunity to use my transferable skills to generate more income on which to live and to make sure that I could cover our modest living expenses, alongside the mortgage on our small house. In hindsight I now see that I had four strategies to ensure my survival in my "retirement ministry":

- I sought to enhance my skills as a counsellor/psychotherapist;
- I took up opportunities and invitations to use the skills and insights developed during my parochial ministry and ministerial training and continuing professional development;
- I was determined to enhance the professional status of counselling in primary care;
- I needed to pray the Office, to study, and to remain somehow connected to the Church (I believe that at this time I felt I belonged far less than a lay person).

I also had the naive belief that the Church might avail itself of my newly acquired skills. Sadly, until recently, in what I consider to be my genuine retirement, the Church showed no interest whatsoever in my welfare or in what I might be doing.

PRIEST-AT-LARGE

To develop my skills as a counsellor/psychotherapist I managed to become qualified on the first course in counselling supervision at York St John University. I had already obtained my qualifications in Human Relations Education, Education Design, Consultancy, and all forms of Group Work, and these complemented my therapy skills and practice. Furthermore, I took the opportunity to do a course in Interpersonal Psychodynamic Psychotherapy at Manchester Royal Infirmary. Naturally, in accordance with my professional practice, I was also receiving supervision for my work for about three hours each week.

The opportunities for other occasional work seemed to come quite easily. I quickly became a regular presenter at all the local postgraduate medical institutes in and around the Manchester area, doing training in bereavement and relationship issues, in the benefits of professional supervision, or in the importance of good counselling skills. I was invited to be consultant to the Cancer Support Centre in Bradford, training counsellors and looking at organizational issues. Occasional lectures at universities also seemed to come my way. They all supplemented my income.

I was extremely interested in the development of counselling and psychotherapy in primary care in general and in the north-west of England in particular, and soon I became chair of the local branch of the professional Association. This brought me to the attention of the national professional Association, which soon began to use me as a resource.

These four strands developed over the following years. I felt very much a "priest-at-large". There was never any denial of my priesthood and I began to learn how to express my ministry in a very different world. Certainly, most of my ministry involved pastoral care for clients/patients and my colleagues, along with a deep concern for this expression of therapy and its development. All the while I attended the local church as a member of the congregation with my wife and to my joy after some time actually developed deeper friendships with people who had formerly been parishioners. The professional distance that I had often felt and, in a sense, used as a parish priest diminished, and I slowly learned to be a priest and a person in a different way. My priesthood was quietly acknowledged by colleagues and patients alike in the medical centre where I worked and later in the University of Salford where I lectured part-time and helped develop and initiate their master's course in Counselling in Primary Care. This certainly did not seem like retirement, but rather as development, both personal and professional.

At the same time, I felt considerable sadness that the Church had not recognized my ministry in some way or, in a sense, claimed me as their own. I was going through all the stages of bereavement, as others felt that I had somehow "left the Church". There were feelings of shock, anger, confusion, arguing about my situation with myself, and finally a sort of resolution, a reconciliation, as to my situation. All of these feelings were disordered and arose in me from time to time, just as they often do in a bereaved person. Had I committed a sort of suicide in daring to move into a different and innovative ministry? It was a crisis of identity that persisted for many a year. I had moved away from "the ark of Christ's Church" to swim and make my life and express my priesthood in a secular sea. During all of this time, I was worshipping, praying, watching and observing the Church that I love with a keen interest and all, as it were, from the sidelines. Had I sidelined myself, or had I been sidelined? There was certainly little curiosity about me or my expression of priesthood from any church authority.

In the year 2001 (aged fifty-six), I was invited by the British Association for Counselling and Psychotherapy (BACP) to be their first Lead Advisor in Healthcare Counselling and Psychotherapy. This meant that I had an open brief to advise and inform the Association on all professional matters concerning counselling and psychotherapy in all healthcare settings. BACP is based in Rugby, and I lived in Lancashire, so it was agreed that I worked from home with a personal assistant based in Rugby. The National Health Service in all the four nations of the UK has been in a state of constant change for many years, and nowhere more so than in primary care and the area of common mental health problems. I became the field officer, so to speak, in representing those who wanted to know more about the impact of counselling and counsellors in all types of healthcare settings. I travelled widely, from Shetland, where I helped to establish their Primary Care Counselling Service, down to the far South West, and into Northern Ireland, and on occasion the Republic of Ireland.

I was called on to make presentations and representations, and to be involved in some of the work of the National Institute for Health and Clinical Excellence. I ran training events. I sat on the examining boards of various universities in relation to qualifications for counselling and psychotherapy. I addressed meetings of counsellors and psychotherapists, hospital chaplains, doctors, psychologists, and psychiatrists concerning their issues, their needs, and their practice. I became an editor of the BACP *Healthcare Counselling and Psychotherapy Journal* and was asked to write articles and chapters in various publications. All the time, I maintained a clinical practice for one day a week in the medical centre where I began this work and continued to have supervision. One of the additional tasks that came my way was the monthly supervision of the Ethical Helpline Team, a group of people established by BACP who were available by telephone to help to facilitate the ethical thinking of counsellors and psychotherapists who had various ethical dilemmas. My theological formation (which is another unconventional story) had apparently equipped me to have some knowledge and skill in applied ethics.

In short, I was a busy person but now employed, and so the burden of self-employment was lifted from me. Is this really retirement, I ask myself? As far as the Church of England was concerned who was I? An erring priest? A maverick priest? Certainly I was as far as the diocesan mailing was concerned, and I was a "retired priest". Life was exciting, interesting, and constantly demanding in so many ways. There was freedom for innovation and creativity, development, leadership, and a breadth of opportunity. I acknowledge that I also felt this about my ministry as a parish priest and yet by daring to step outside the official structures of the Church of England I seemed to blossom even further through this experience. I seemed to be able to reach parts that other priests did not reach. It often came as a surprise to various NHS officials and Government representatives to realize that they were dealing with a priest, and there were frequent opportunities to witness to my faith and belief.

One of my interests throughout has been the relationship between counselling and psychotherapy and pastoral care and spirituality. BACP has different professional sections within the Association (such as Universities counselling, Schools and Colleges counselling, Coaching, Children and Young People) and alongside Healthcare (where I had risen through the ranks of the volunteer executive) there was a section devoted to counselling and psychotherapy and pastoral care and spirituality. I had always been a member of this section alongside my healthcare interest; at Association headquarters in Rugby, because it was no secret that I was a priest, I became unofficially consulted on all matters in these areas. In this busy so-called "retired" life, this was a fascinating area and naturally appealed to my ecumenical and theological thinking, as well as to my interest in other faiths and in the spirituality of agnostics and atheists. Apologetics has always appealed to me in all its forms.

In 2011, I was sixty-five years old, and for some time I had been thinking about retirement from my BACP work. Since 2004, I had extended my role by also being the Lead Advisor for Spiritual and Pastoral Care in Counselling and Psychotherapy alongside my healthcare position. In 2007, I voluntarily relinquished my healthcare position but retained my Spiritual and Pastoral Care role. This position was fascinating, and I recall marketing myself to all Anglican and Roman Catholic diocesan bishops and to leaders of faith communities of all types.

My model of working had become a template for other lead advisors to be appointed for all the differing sections of the Association and indeed for the different countries of the UK. I was part of a specialist team. Our family had moved to live and work in Cornwall, and about a year earlier I had asked if I could relocate to Cornwall and still continue with my job. To my surprise the Association agreed and allowed me to remain in my employment. To continue to do a national job covering the whole of the UK from West Cornwall was a challenge in itself. I was asked when I wanted to retire, and I indicated that I would like to continue until I was sixty-six years old.

RECOGNITION IN RETIREMENT

On arriving in Cornwall, within a few months, a curious incident occurred. I had decided that I would attend a "Celebration of Wholeness and Healing" at Truro Cathedral. This was out of professional interest and also because of the opportunity to meet an old acquaintance, Bishop Jack Nicholls, formerly of Sheffield. In the event, I not only met him but also met the current Bishop of Truro who was still to be installed. He happened to be sitting in the same pew and was keeping a low profile. I recognized him and introduced myself and he shared his concern about the general wellbeing of clergy in the diocese and those he would be called upon to ordain. I said that I may be able to help given my experience in ministry and in psychotherapy and related matters. I was very near my retirement, and since that meeting my ministry has, in what I would call my proper retirement, developed apace.

It was not long before the bishop was asking me to see clergy with a variety of emotional, pastoral, and psychological issues. As might be expected there was often a spiritual and pastoral component involved. Since that time, I have been employed, voluntarily and otherwise, to offer various interventions to assist my clergy colleagues and sometimes their parishes at the same time. This has always been in close collaboration with the bishop and/or archdeacons. The majority of the work has been confidential, although not all can be hidden. The amount of work is sometimes a matter of concern, particularly to my wife. Am I retired or not? A Roman Catholic priest remarked to me that, as he saw it for a married priest, retirement could be very much like a gift to his or her partner. I think this is a good observation. Years of not being physically together in the same pew or adjacent seat during worship does not always enhance a relationship for those who have been joined together in the sacrament of holy matrimony; retirement can restore something of that sacramental unity.

As my unique ministry in retirement has developed, so have my concerns for some aspects of the Church. The interventions with and for clergy that I have made at the request of my bishop I often felt could have been avoided to the benefit of everyone. Increasingly it became apparent to me that some of my colleagues were in distress in various ways because, perhaps, they did not have the requisite gifts or characteristics that are needed within their personalities. Sometimes unresolved issues from their pasts would resurface inappropriately; at other times there were hidden motives in becoming a priest that were not entirely wholesome or beneficial in ministry. Again, the research on the personality of clergy indicates that many are "tender-minded", and they can lack the necessary resilience. Theologically, spiritually, and sexually there may be unresolved issues and inevitably, as they say, "submarines surface" with often unforeseen and sometimes disastrous consequences.

During my work for BACP, I became acquainted with the work of St Luke's Centre in Manchester. This Roman Catholic centre does a thoroughgoing analysis (psychological, spiritual, social, theological, physical, and sexual) of those desirous of being ordained or wishing to enter the religious life before training commences. I suggested that we needed to be more thorough in assessment and discernment within the diocese before a candidate even went to a Bishop's Advisory Panel (BAP), loosely along the lines of the St Luke's programme. There was no intention to create a monochrome type of candidate but rather to give help before training for ordained ministry to inform the decisions of the Diocesan Director of Ordinands and the Diocesan Bishop. Inevitably I became involved in developing a pre-BAP psycho-social interview which has proved to be useful as part of our diocesan vocation process of discernment. This now runs alongside days where potential candidates can be observed in group work interactions before going to a BAP.

Another area of concern resulting from my consideration of interventions on behalf of the senior staff was that some difficult situations were often contributed to as a consequence of a priest's apparent isolation. If anything could be done to alleviate this, then my colleagues may be more wholesome. Having previously, when a rural dean, initiated ways of promoting collegiality with some success with a colleague, I endeavoured to influence openness and sharing in our local deanery chapter. This has borne fruit and gone even further. As we shared our situations with one another and those of other colleagues, we resolved to submit a resolution to the Diocesan Synod called "Never Alone", where the chapter strongly suggested that support and encouragement in a number of ways should become part of diocesan structures and policy. This was backed by some startling research within the diocese which indicated the depth of isolation experienced by a considerable number of clergy. A working party, which included myself, was formed and the proposal accepted. The project is currently developing. There may be developments nationally as a result (see Stuart-White, Vaughan-Wilson, Eatock, Muskell and Village, 2018).

My forays into encouraging collegiality, alongside supervision, support, and group work, as in most helping professions these days, has also resulted in working with a colleague to develop further what are known as "practice-based learning groups". These have taken place in various forms in the diocese. The parallel Roman Catholic Diocese of Plymouth is also using me on a regular basis in a supervisory role and to run "practice-based learning groups". These groups are similar to the Balint Groups that are popular with GPs. They originated in the Diocese of Bristol where some original research was done by Mary Travis (2008) in her article "Supporting clergy in postmodern ministry".

A VISION FOR RETIRED CLERGY

My observations of my colleagues who are also "retired" both encourages me and causes me concern, especially as they could soon exceed the number of stipendiary clergy nationally and already have done so in our diocese. I see that the majority continue in ministry and often preside at services but do little else. I also recognize that many are grieving the ministry that they once had and sometimes need support and understanding. They can also be inclined to interfere in congregations. Sometimes we retired priests can be extremely reactionary and hold back the ministry of current stipendiary clergy, because there has been little recognition by us that times are changing in so many ways. Others can be extremely generous of their time and skills in ministry. Sometimes we are gloriously out of touch with the Church, theology, liturgy, and current culture, to the point where we reinforce a view of the Church that is not helpful to our stipendiary colleagues.

I could go on. I would love to see a situation where retired clergy are only given PTO when they can promise to evidence their continuous professional development, attend chapter and work positively with stipendiary and self-supporting colleagues, and resolve to indicate exactly what duties they are able to perform, be it liturgically or in other ways, such as mentoring. All of this needs to be reviewed every three or so years, until full retirement from active ministry. Other professions would demand nothing less, and I believe that our Lord and the Church of God into which we have been ordained deserve as much. Our priestly work of intercession and worship and service in general would, of course, continue.

I conclude with my initial question, "When did my retirement begin?", which has now to be reframed into "when will my ministry in retirement end?" Perhaps when I cease to be competent, up to date, when I am physically incapable of doing what I do now and very importantly when my wife especially, and others, give me feedback to say that enough is enough and I am called to be myself as priest and person differently yet again. I have been greatly blessed in my retirement to date.

REFERENCES

Stuart-White, B., Vaughan-Wilson, J., Eatock, J., Muskett, J. A., and Village, A. (2018), "Isolation among rural clergy: Exploring experiences and solutions in one diocese", *Rural Theology* 16, pp. 65–79

Travis, M. (2008), "Supporting clergy in postmodern ministry", *Practical Theology* 1, pp. 95–130.

6. AND SOME HAVE RETIREMENT THRUST UPON THEM

Peter Knibbs

The service at Newcastle Cathedral was so special, and I felt so proud. It was 3 October 2015 and my wife Yvonne was being licensed as a reader after what had been three years of hard work for her. She began her training in the Diocese of Truro when I was priest-in-charge of a cluster of eight rural congregations. The post was a privilege for me and also a challenge, but after four years of working through change and building up a good team of colleagues, the ministry was starting to prosper. Yvonne and I were looking forward to a shared ministry as her strong pastoral skills and her gift as a patient listener complement my strengths and enhance my weaknesses.

AN UNEXPECTED TURN OF EVENTS

We had previously lived in Newcastle upon Tyne, and two of our three sons live there with four of our grandchildren. Yvonne's father was living with us in Cornwall, and his level of dependency was ever increasing as he lives with Parkinson's Disease. We had always imagined retirement in the North East (itself a beautiful part of the country) and decided that, despite the beauty and charm of Cornwall, we wanted to grow old close to our sons and their families. The decision to move from Cornwall was accelerated by my father-in-law's worsening health and one year almost to the day before Yvonne's licensing, I was inducted as vicar of St Mary the Virgin, Monkseaton, looking forward to perhaps eight to ten years of a "traditional" role as parish priest. I was fifty-nine years old.

The change of course for Yvonne midway through training was a challenge, but the Lindisfarne Training Partnership were extremely helpful and supportive, as were the staff team at the new church, one of whom was an experienced reader herself, offering wise mentorship. For my part, it was a glorious time. A single congregation that I inherited in good heart with no major problems to solve. A strong congregation and staff team all with a desire to grow spiritually and reach out with God's love. I took a personal strategic decision to spend twelve months getting to know people, learning names, and getting to know how the various groups within the church worked. There had been a previous faculty approved for comprehensive internal reordering, and during that first year I was able to oversee the works and guide the congregation through three months of mild disruption worshipping in the adjacent church hall.

I had not always been a stipendiary priest. I studied dentistry at university and worked in various roles (general dental practice, research and university lecturer, and latterly in Cornwall in NHS management). These experiences had equipped me well for the multifaceted work as a full-time vicar, and I felt positive. I was enjoying good health, an ideal weight for my size, and had never felt fitter as I cycled around the lovely seaside suburbs of my new North Tyneside parish.

One week after Yvonne's licensing, one year after my own induction service, four days before the bishop was coming to celebrate the opening of the newly reordered church, I was enjoying a cup of tea in the church hall with the congregation after the main Sunday service. I suddenly felt severe pain in my chest. There had been no obvious reason for the onset, but I knew I was experiencing something unlike I had ever felt before. I sought my wife and the relative privacy of a side room, and a general medical practitioner in the congregation hurried to my side as we called an ambulance. Within forty-five minutes, after a blue light drive, my wife and I were received at Newcastle's Freeman Hospital, a regional cardio-thoracic centre of world renown. A new chapter of my life and the life of my family was beginning.

APPRECIATING SUPPORT

I could write extensively about the great medical care and the various procedures and tests, but I am aware that I can easily become a "heart attack" bore as I talk in too great detail about a subject so dear to my heart. The scope of this piece is more focused on clergy retirement, and so I hope now to skim over aspects of my medical condition while detailing some of my experiences of a retirement journey.

In mentioning brilliant, loving support from family and friends, I am sure I echo the experiences of many who like me have suffered the blow of unexpected illness. Those I love and who love me appreciate how special they are and how much I value them even without specific mention in this piece, and to focus on those loved ones might again stray from the remit of this chapter. I want, therefore, to mention the support received from the people at St Mary's, the diocese, and indeed the national Church as being of more likely interest to this topic of retirement for Anglican clergy.

One member of the staff team followed the ambulance carrying my wife and me to the hospital. She stayed with my wife and my family for most of the afternoon, offering love and quiet, prayerful support. Later that afternoon, the archdeacon visited once I was settled into a bed after the emergency procedure. We later joked about his visit, as I was high on morphine at the time and he saw an extravert side to me that is not often on show. Throughout my illness and recovery, he has been an encouraging friend, adding special value to my thinking and decision-making as he too is a survivor of serious heart problems.

Soon after my return home, I was visited by our bishop, and he too paid regular visits throughout the weeks and months that followed. He arranged for his pastoral adviser to see me to offer emotional and psychological support. That wise and experienced priest also had experienced heart problems, and so empathy was strong as we chatted and he helped me put some order to the jumble of emotions and decisions that I was facing. I was visited by the area dean and the former area dean, and received amazing support from the staff team at St Mary's. The congregation were exemplary in their sensitivity, only phoning or calling with Yvonne's agreement and only staying a short time so as not to tire me unduly. This level of love and concern across the diocese was all the more amazing to us as we were so new to the diocese and relatively unknown.

The following months were frustrating. Literature about recovery from heart attack is generally upbeat, but any suggestion of a return to work after six weeks proved unrealistic in my case. My heart had been badly damaged when starved of its blood supply and each consultation with the specialists told of further treatment and further waits on NHS lists. I genuinely offered the congregation and staff team the prospect of a return to work three months after the heart attack, but this then slipped to six months due to further necessary procedures, and I write this thirteen months into this illness and still I am not yet cleared as being out of active treatment and therefore ready to consider any future role.

The episode clearly hit me and my family hard, but from soon after my return home, I was determined to return to work. The diocese were most supportive and never once tried to hurry my decision; rather, they were often voices of caution to counter my unrealistic optimism. St Mary's is a busy church. The previous incumbent had established strong networks of lay involvement, but the work of oversight of all the various core groups and task groups was demanding of time and energy, on top of all the other duties of a diligent parish priest. Like many other clergy, I had needed to invest long hours to cope with the demands of the post. I now observed from the sanctuary of the vicarage just how much this was demanding of the staff team, none of whom were stipendiary, who were valiantly offering cover for me in my absence, and like many (I am sure) I was not immune to feelings of guilt and a desire to get back to offer help. The archdeacon especially was urging me to resist these feelings of guilt and to take all necessary time.

Yvonne experienced a range of emotions and the situation was especially complex for her as a newly licensed member of the staff team. She is a very experienced Christian with previous training in spiritual direction and pastoral listening, but settling into the new role as reader should include induction by the incumbent. Instead of induction, she was drawn into the maelstrom of a staff team and a congregation forced to cope with my absence. Initially the staff team counselled her to step back completely from all duty, although she resisted this, arguing that she was not ill and that, although her reader ministry was linked to my ministry, it was independent of it. However, in time the wisdom of the team's initial advice became clear as she struggled with stress, overwork, guilt, grief, rapidly changing circumstances, and worry about my future treatments and prognosis. She soon joined me in the sanctuary of the vicarage as we pondered our futures and licked our wounds.

FACING PRACTICALITIES

My former career in dentistry had provided for us comfortably as a family over the years and we were living in our own home in Cornwall, and remained there with the Bishop of Truro's agreement even when I took early retirement from the NHS to become a stipendiary priest. We put our home on the market once announcements were made about our move to the North East, but we were underwhelmed with interest and agreed to rent the home to a friend's daughter and her partner and their four children. The rental agreement was within their budget and was sufficient to cover our mortgage repayments, so it was a "win-win", but it added complexity as I felt I needed to be honest about this arrangement to the mortgage provider. They granted six months permission to let, but would then increase the interest rate by a further 1.5 per cent. Just before the six-month deadline (and while I was still well), we took advice from a mortgage advisor and remortgaged with a "buy to let" mortgage and (importantly) we took out appropriate mortgage protection insurance both on our lives and for critical illness. The latter is considered by some to be a luxury, but it proved a great benefit to us in the weeks after my heart attack. The insurers paid up in full to clear our mortgage after appropriate medical reports confirmed my heart attack and so we were freed from the potential burden of mortgage repayments. Coincidentally, our tenants had found a property they could afford to buy in Cornwall and so (with some embarrassment due to their knowledge of my recent illness) they gave us notice of their intent to leave.

We pondered seeking new tenants but decided to try again to sell the property and this second time around we had two interested buyers and so were able to secure a good price. The sale was completed four months after the heart attack, leaving us with no mortgage and the full value of the house to invest in a retirement home for our future. At this stage, a return to work was still my hope and intention as we began the exciting process of looking for a property.

Perhaps Yvonne's favourite former home had been a "new build" house in Birmingham not long after my graduation as a dentist, and so we favoured a brand new house, spending time looking at many show homes before settling upon the design and location of a new house for sale six miles up the coast from St Mary's, in the seaside town of Blyth in Northumberland. We had little previous knowledge of Blyth, but nevertheless following prayer and some local research, we decided to make the purchase and the house became ours in March 2016, a cash purchase that proceeded with no problems.

Three weeks before the completion on the new house, I faced further surgery. The consultant had been brutally frank about possible complications. I respect his professional skill, his honesty, and his humour. Knowing I was a clergyman, he explained that if things did go wrong "I would meet my boss sooner than perhaps expected." The humour was welcome, but the message was sobering, and so in the weeks leading up to the surgery, I took pains to make sure most of our money was invested in joint accounts and that Yvonne and my sons were conversant with our finances. I had always been the one in our relationship who had handled the finances. Yvonne had delegated this to me gladly over the years, and she was not too happy about my wishes to clarify everything before my surgery. She viewed this as unnecessary pessimism, while I felt it gave me some comfort to know she would be secure and prepared should my arrival at the pearly gates be unfortunately premature. I survived the surgery, but the procedure did not go according to plan and once again I was facing the prospect of further months of waiting, and further procedures before I would be able to decide if I was fit to return to work.

It has been my practice for many years to say Morning Prayer from *Common Worship: Daily Prayer*, and I include penitential material as part of my morning devotions. There is one confession that reads:

> Most merciful God, Father of our Lord Jesus Christ, we confess
> that we have sinned in thought, word and deed. We have not loved
> you with our whole heart. We have not loved our neighbours as

ourselves. In your mercy forgive what we have been, help us to amend what we are, and direct what we shall be; that we may do justly, love mercy, and walk humbly with you our God. Amen.

Not long after my heart attack, this prayer struck me deeply in a way that God's word sometimes does. The latter phrases from Micah 6:8 spoke loudly to me about how I should approach the new realities of my life and my decision-making.

The first influential phrase has been "love mercy". Indeed, the care, compassion, and time given me by so many people has certainly been full of mercy. I have also had to be merciful to myself. My father died quite early in my adult life, but he was always loving; he remains a man who taught me a great deal and whom I respect. One of his mantras to me in childhood was "Good, better, best and never rest until your good is better and your better, best". For much of my life at school, at university, in my professional career, and then as a priest I have been driven to do my best, to work hard, to please others, and to achieve success. This ethic is deeply engrained in my psyche.

Before my conversion in early adult life, my ambition for success, status, and wealth were powerful driving forces. After I started to take my faith in Christ seriously on weekdays as well as on Sundays, the power of the ambition was the same, but hopefully (most of the time) the focus was more on working for the good of God's kingdom and God's mission, not my own selfish desires. I am sure that a psychologist could have a rich time delving into these complexities of my being, but one constant has been a strong sense of obligation and an easy adoption of feelings of guilt if I perceive I have let others down. Now, placed in a situation beyond my control where I have certainly fallen short of people's hopes of me, I must be merciful and gracious to myself, allowing myself this frailty without guilt or recrimination.

The phrase "walk humbly" has been a source of much personal reflection. Serious illness strips away so many of life's normalities. There is loss of status, control, identity, ability, and self-worth. I imagine that these are aspects for many people of their experience of retirement, but sudden illness forces them into prominence with acute brutality and without the courtesy of an ability to choose the timing of new circumstances.

However, a choice remains, namely to accept the new reality or to rail against it. The former demands humility.

Walking humbly involves offering the arm uncomplainingly to the nurse taking yet more blood samples. Walking humbly involves allowing others to care, especially in practical ways. How hard to watch Yvonne carry heavy shopping bags, while I walk beside her empty-handed. Walking humbly involves not getting involved when my curate plans things her way and not perhaps the way I would have chosen. Walking humbly involves accepting graciously when my one son asks another son to come round to sit with me in Yvonne's absence when the first son has to go back to work. I might easily fill the allotted word count of this chapter recalling the times I have had to remind myself of my need for humility. I hope that I have never been a prideful man, but how painful this journey to seek growth of humility.

Then there is "do justly". No great scope to foster major injustice while convalescing in a vicarage. But scope nevertheless, and none more so than in my decision-making regarding my future ministry. Although health is a very personal affair, I decided to be as open as possible with the people of St Mary's and so tried to keep people informed about each stage of my recovery and the implications for my return to work. When the procedure in March 2016 was not as straightforward as I had hoped, and the outcome remained uncertain, I decided that acting justly meant setting St Mary's free to seek a new vicar.

I am sure the diocese and the congregation would have been prepared to wait longer, and I was never in doubt of the diocesan commitment to me. Even as the six-month period of full stipend elapsed, I was reassured of the bishop's discretion to keep paying me in full. But somehow to me, acting justly meant letting go. I had loved the people, the work, and the opportunities, and I had hoped to remain at St Mary's until such time as I planned retirement, but I felt that I should make my own hopes and wishes subservient to the greater good of the congregation and the staff team. I talked to the archdeacon about ill-health retirement a few days after the surgical procedure had suggested a long road still ahead for my treatment.

Financially, my clergy pension was always going to be as a supplement to my NHS pension. I was fortunate to build up a pension fund in the NHS for thirty-three years, and based on my final salary this proves sufficient for a comfortable, if not lavish, retirement. The monthly pension from the Clergy Pension Board is not big and would be much less if ill-health retirement were declined. More importantly though, the tax-free lump sum was significantly improved with the award of ill-health retirement, compared to retirement of my own choice some seven years before the usual age. In this regard also, I have been treated well by the Church of England and the Diocese of Newcastle. After less than two months of seeking medical reports and confirmations from the diocese, I was granted ill-health retirement as from 31 May 2016, and was then able to act justly and offer my resignation to the bishop to enable St Mary's to begin again the process of finding a new incumbent.

THEOLOGICAL CHALLENGES AND FUTURE OPPORTUNITIES

Not long after my heart attack, three separate Christian friends, whose spirituality and wisdom I respect, sent me the short text from Jeremiah 29:11:

> For surely I know the plans I have for you, says the Lord, plans
> for your welfare and not for harm, to give you a future with hope.

I am from an evangelical background, and the Bible has always been, and remains, an important pillar of my faith. The popular "wall plaque" verse sent to me by my three friends has in the past encouraged me in major life decisions, but on receiving it in the context of my illness, I found more challenge than encouragement. The context of the verse is found in a longer passage where Jeremiah is writing to exiles, explaining that their banishment was from God, but that later restoration will also come from God. Is this what my friends (or God through them) were telling me, that somehow I was banished like Israel and Judah were banished for their sins? Do God's plans for people include illness and disaster?

I pondered these verses out of respect for my friends (and the afore-mentioned intention towards humility) but found little comfort or clarity.

My reflections led me to acknowledge that we live in a shaky, frail world alongside shaky and frail people, and that things happen as a result of natural consequences, human actions, and our freedom to choose.

My lifestyle according to current medical wisdom would have placed me as low risk of a heart attack (as confirmed ironically three weeks before my attack when a routine check at my doctor's surgery scored me as less than five per cent risk). Perhaps my choice of working long hours in a pressured role contributed. Perhaps it was my genetic makeup, although I have no strong family history of heart disease. But does God give clergy heart attacks as part of God's good plan for their ministry and welfare? I shall only be sure when I see clearly through the glass that is presently only murkily illuminated.

We moved into our new home in Blyth in April 2016, and at the end of that month I had the joy, sorrow, and privilege of preaching and presiding for the last time at St Mary's, Monkseaton. We have settled well into our new parish of St Cuthbert's, initially as parishioners, but quickly the diocese agreed to license Yvonne as reader here. Our new diocesan bishop met me soon after my decision to retire and has granted me permission to officiate, but with an invitation to talk further after all my treatment is completed about how my ministry might progress in accordance with what I might be able to offer.

Unexpectedly (certainly for Yvonne and me) a few months after we joined the church, the incumbent of St Cuthbert's who had welcomed us so warmly announced a move to Australia and left at the end of September 2016, leaving St Cuthbert's in vacancy while I write this chapter. I have been able to help in various ways, including preaching, presiding, and offering advice to the two churchwardens who are now doing sterling work holding things together. This role, albeit temporary until we find a new vicar, has filled me with new hope and purpose.

Next week, I face further surgery that will hopefully take me to the end of treatment and into rehabilitation. I cannot say what this might mean in terms of ministry in my retirement. I cannot say if this now feels like a godly plan for my welfare, not my harm; but a mentor and wise friend, in the early days of my stipendiary ministry, once described a situation as having God's fingerprint on it. It does seem as though there is a divine fingerprint on our situation now. We feel privileged to serve at St Cuthbert's; we are enjoying our new home and discovering all that Blyth and Northumberland has to offer. I have been forced to reflect on my life and ambition and learn some hard lessons about humility, justice, and mercy. The reality check of serious illness helps to put so much into perspective and demands serious consideration about the truly important things in life.

I write this final paragraph as a post-script a week after my latest, and hopefully final, heart surgery. I now have a defibrillator fitted beneath my skin over my left breast like a small boot polish tin breaking the former contours of my chest. A sophisticated electronic device with tendrils reaching down into the chambers of my heart, hopefully a benign friend ready to act as an angel of life if it detects a life-threatening heart rhythm, but also, in some cases, a mischievous metallic imp with potential to shock me unnecessarily should its circuits overreact to some misread increased heart rate. I hope after a review next month to pass from treatment to rehabilitation and the building of the next phase of my life and ministry: grandparenting, helping out at local churches, and perhaps even golf lessons. Or perhaps this next chapter will be penned with unknown new opportunities and challenges by our wonderful God of surprises. Many choose the circumstances of their retirement, while I had mine thrust upon me. I cannot really pretend that I am content with the timing and nature of my retirement, but I have no discontent being an Anglican clergyman in this place at this time: a recipient of the love and practical support of those who are charged with offering care to the pastors as well as to the flock.

7.　A SUBSTITUTE PRIEST?

David Jennings

It was August 2016, and the retirement experience had been but two years and a bit. We had taken our son, daughter-in-law, and three grandsons to Brugge for a brief holiday. The youngest grandson, Niall, aged nine, asked to be taken to see the swans on the lake. On leaving the hotel, he suggested that we call first to my favourite bar. I am impressed by his perception and love for his grandfather. While at the bar, he asked why I retired at sixty-five plus when I could have continued as rector of the parish of Burbage with Aston Flamville until I was seventy. He then told me that I was now just a "substitute priest". Perception again, but laced with a criticism. The beer helped the subsequent conversation with a very cheeky nine-year-old.

I was ordained in 1974 in Worcester Cathedral to serve my title in the very large parish of Halesowen in the Dudley Deanery. In 1977, I left the parish and became director of a multi-faith project in Handsworth, Birmingham, working with the late Professor John Hick, and assistant priest in one of the local churches. From there I went on to be the Bishop of Leicester's Community Relations Chaplain and parish priest of a mining parish in North West Leicestershire, while also being a local councillor. In 1987, I went to Burbage, first as priest-in-charge and then as rector, where I remained until I retired in 2014. In 2003, I was made an Honorary Canon and Canon Theologian in 2010, a position I continue to hold in retirement.

PLANNING WELL AHEAD FOR RETIREMENT

Part of my many life experiences include being a local councillor, serving as chair of the local authority's policy committee, and being a partner in the family wholesale newsagent business. These business, political, and financial experiences convinced me of the need to make adequate preparations for retirement, many years ahead. The business enabled us to purchase properties throughout the period of ministry. Over the years, these were sold, sometimes with a profit, but also occasionally with a loss. In 1998, at the maturity of several endowment policies, we purchased what we thought would be a retirement home in the Lake District. This was a good decision because we and the family enjoyed many good holidays in a very beautiful location, and it enabled me to concentrate on reading and writing. However, as retirement loomed, we realized that with our children, including our severely disabled daughter, living in the East Midlands, we would spend most of our retirement life on the M6 motorway. We therefore began to consider a retirement home in Leicestershire, purchased with the sale of the Lake District flat and legacies from both sets of deceased parents. The privileged position of already owning a property and of receiving the beneficence of deceased parents did not escape us, not least as we compared our situation with that of many other clergy couples.

Although there was an inevitable and perhaps understandable wrench from a parish in which we had lived and served for twenty-seven years, the purchase and move to a new home was not problematic. The purchase price of £200,000, with a small bridging loan until the Lake District property was sold, was easily within our budget. A smaller home required some painful downsizing, including several valued books, and the discovery of many forgotten items in the rectory lofts. However, the retirement house was in an attractive village with all the necessary amenities and situated close to the local canal. It is often remarked that when retiring, one should ensure walking distance to a doctor. A further advantage to the home we chose was that it had three floors which ensured constant energy in accessing the living room, the bedrooms, and most importantly, the study. For ourselves the purchasing of a new property for retirement and the leaving of a large rectory was not a significant problem. The key, I suppose, was forward planning and the recognition that retirement needs to be planned and programmed well in advance of the day when one must move.

A DIFFICULT PARISH

If I was to identify a problem, frustration and disappointment as a retired priest, such occurred with what was subsequently experienced. The parish we retired to had an incumbent who had been my former curate. It was, as is all too often stated, a difficult parish, and he did not easily fit into the role of rector of a conservative middle-of-the-road benefice with fourteen churches. Such, of course, would be a challenge for any energetic and enthusiastic priest, but my former colleague, immediately after appointment, was diagnosed with bowel cancer, and stated that he was gay and in a relationship with a former Roman Catholic priest. The parish had also recently received a significant legacy, and not a few parishioners had very clear ideas as to how such should be administered and who should be responsible for the same.

As my former colleague was recovering from surgery and depression, the then bishop asked if I would take responsibility and address some of the many problems that existed within the benefice. Having only just retired from a significant and very large parish and being somewhat unsure as to how to continue to exercise priestly ministry, the opportunity to continue in some form of ministry seemed attractive and affirming. Although receiving support and ostensible authority from the bishop, as well as the archdeacon and diocesan secretary, it was not the same as having the responsibility and authority which goes with being an incumbent. With the retirement of the bishop and resistance from within the parish to agreed changes and challenges, matters very quickly began to unravel. Apart from the desperate situation left by my former curate as he moved on to another position within the Church, it was clear that disgruntled and aggressive parishioners were only too aware that my position was temporary and that a new incumbent was being sought. Personal verbal and media attacks were unwelcome and challenged the support of the diocese during what was now an episcopal interregnum.

It also became clear, not only from my own experience, which included an all too lengthy interregnum in my former parish, compounded by the lethargy and procedural inadequacies of a private patron (an Oxbridge college), that prolonged interregna were not beneficial for large and significant parishes. I have concluded that in such instances, the appointment of an interim priest with the full authority that would appertain to an incumbent is a desirable and perhaps necessary development. With greater financial accountability to the diocese, the Charity Commission and HMRC being required and demanded, parishes cannot be left just to fend for themselves. This, of course, increasingly applies to issues concerning safeguarding. Such a role could easily be given to a retired priest with an honorarium, and the necessary episcopal approval and authority.

A CRISIS OF IDENTITY

As well as financial, housing, and vocational implications for retirement, there is the confused issue concerning identity. At one of our many pub lunch meetings, and just prior to retirement for both, the then bishop suggested that retirement could result in a personal crisis of identity. As a convinced socialist with a Catholic outlook, I wanted to reject this suggestion. I have never regarded individuality as a defining and determining form of identity. It was with a degree of superciliousness that I suggested to the bishop that such a crisis would only be experienced if it was confused with that of status. I was conscious that the bishop was paying for the lunch and that perhaps my comment was disrespectful, unkind, and unwarranted. The bishop was correct, and priestly identity is not only important but impacts upon self-understanding and experience. Forty years, or however long one has been ordained, as a priest cannot be eliminated or expunged by the experience of retirement, and the consequence can be a crisis of identity. I have subsequently apologized to the bishop, but have pondered his words and shared them with him at his own retirement.

Priesthood is not a function or a job that is given with certain expectations, namely a job description, although some changes in the

Church seem to be moving in that direction. It is an indelible gift, a sacramental charism, that cannot be lightly or wantonly discarded at a certain age or upon receipt of a pension. The question remains as to how the priestly identity and reality can be expressed and exercised in retirement. There is likely to be an ecclesiological distinction between different views concerning the ministerial priesthood, not least within the Church of England which contains and holds together significant different and differing views, both of the Church and ministry. For some, the ministry is purely and exclusively functional. Those who hold to this view and understanding are also predisposed to minimise any distinction that the ordained ministry may have with that of the role of the laity, whether exercised as a defined ministry or just as is often mistakenly identified as the "priesthood of all believers". There is no New Testament phrase that makes such an assertion, and the passage often quoted from 1 Peter 2 uses the definition of priesthood in a generic sense of a shared priesthood as indicative of the community of believers, a holy priesthood or royal priesthood, God's own people, and has no bearing or relevance to an ordained ministry. To use these verses as in some respect referencing the ordained ministry is to commit a categorical error which does little to enhance an understanding of ministry, both ordained and lay.

The view often cited in this respect has an impact for a practical outworking of the priestly vocation while in retirement. Put simply, the question is to what extent is the priest still a priest in retirement, and furthermore how can such be given tangible expression within both the life of the community in which one is located and the diocese? Even the rather mundane matter of wearing the clerical collar can become an issue when confronted with the often-cited expression, "but I thought you were retired?" At a time when the Church is becoming increasingly reliant on the services and ministry of the retired, there is a case for a form of parity of esteem, and more importantly for an adequate expression of the continuity of the priestly vocation and identity. For those of us with a Catholic disposition and understanding of the charism given at ordination, it is of crucial importance that who we are is contiguous with what we have been, and can perhaps be best expressed in the somewhat simplistic statement, "once a priest always a priest". Retirement does not effect a change, but rather confirms the identity. Whether this necessitates regular attendance at ecclesiastical meetings becomes an open question and requires an individual response, but the same is true for those exercising a pre-retirement ministry. While priestly solidarity is to be valued and displayed, such is not dependent on attendance at a Deanery Synod or Diocesan Synod.

CHANGING CONTEXTS OF FRIENDS AND FINANCE

As part of the training given at theological college it was suggested that it was not a good thing to form friendships within the parish. There is a clear and good reason behind this practical approach to parochial ministry. The risk of the perception of privileged access to the parish priest, and the risk of there being a clique, does not enable a dispassionate pastoral exercising of ministry. There is also the likelihood of bias concerning the more practical application of parish life, not least concerning significant matters of finance and structures. The obvious difficulty associated with this ministerial practice is the possibility of isolation. While this was not a problem for me, my wife found it difficult and demanding. Whatever relationships were experienced in the parish, and at whatever level, the problem became more acute upon retirement. The practice and expectation that there should be no further contact with the former parish can be a demanding and burdensome requirement, and especially for the clergy partner who then must forge new relationships and new friendships. At a certain age, such is easier said than done, but it is an issue for those just entering retirement and we have been very mindful that, following a problematic interregnum, we should not inhibit a new parish priest in her or his ministry.

Matters concerning pension and tax issues have also been at the forefront of retirement ministry. Having always been somewhat meticulous concerning our financial affairs, and believing strongly in the payment of due taxes, it has been necessary not only to keep precise details of income received in respect of fees and interregna services, but also to ensure correct advice concerning legitimate expenditure relating to the conduct of continued ministry. We have been fortunate in having the services of a financial advisor without charge who completes and forwards our self-assessment tax declarations. There may be some retired priests who are not so fortunate, and there may be some who thereby fail to make a proper declaration to HMRC. With the increased use of retired clergy conducting services, it is possible that HMRC might one day be tempted to examine the situation of payments and fees received in retirement.

There is also the question concerning the adequacy of pension. Most would perhaps suggest that such always falls short of what one might expect or hope for. However, the fact that the pension is non-contributory is clearly a considerable benefit. The temptation to reduce benefits further should be resisted and perhaps active trade union membership would prove helpful in this regard. One of the justifications for a relatively low stipend was the deferred benefit to be received through a pension. If there is a further reduction in pension benefit, then a significant increase in stipend would be necessary to enable "top up" payments or a separate pension provision. Such should be benchmarked against a comparable occupation with similar responsibilities. The salary of a headteacher has often been quoted. There is perhaps much more that the Church could do, both before and during retirement, in supporting and advising clergy in matters concerning pensions, tax, and benefits. A good example could be the availability of working tax credits, which we received for a good proportion of stipendiary ministry.

VISION FOR RETIREMENT IN A CHANGING CHURCH

Changes taking place in the Church are likely to have an impact on priests who were trained at least thirty years ago, and within a residential theological college. The emphasis was often on both a liturgical and pastoral parochial ministry. This contrasts with emphasis today on "fresh expressions" and on placing numbers above all else as indicative of ministry. Some seek to establish forms of ministerial practice that bear little resemblance to and have little respect for parochial boundaries and for the ministry of others who may exercise a different style within the Church of England. While such may be a natural development of the Church concerned with decline and loss of influence, for many retired priests, including myself, it can be a depressing trajectory that challenges and undermines much that was taught and practised in a previous generation. This concern is not to undermine current trends, but to point out a further aspect of the experience and outlook of some retired priests. A wider recognition of, if not sympathy for, a past and valid form of ministry, based on pastoral care and service within a parish to all without fear or favour, might be a welcome experience for those in retirement.

For some priests a form of continued recognition and appointment would be an advantage in the early years and months of retirement. This may not be always possible, but it could be considered by the diocese. I have been fortunate in that the previous bishop extended my appointment as canon theologian through to the age of seventy-one, and I remain a member of the cathedral chapter. Such is a form of affirmation and a recognition of continued priestly ministry. The ability to serve as chaplain to the High Sheriff also enabled a continued sense both of ministry and identity, although the position was only for one year. In addition, I have been able to continue as chair of two local charities which has helped to retain a sense of purpose and engagement outside of the constraints of the ecclesiastical world.

In summary, I believe we have been fortunate in our retirement home and I was mindful of the need to prepare for that day when alternative accommodation to the parsonage house would be required. Because not all have been as fortunate, there is an argument, to prevent unnecessary anxiety and the limitation of choice in respect of a future home, for provision to be made at the beginning of ministry through the possibility and availability of Church-provided low-cost mortgages. This would enable the priest to be, as is often quoted, on the property ladder. There would be the further advantage of both a rental income and the benefit of increased value and return, over a period of time. Furthermore, there is the pressing need for the Church to address the issue of continued priestly identity. The vocation, made tangible through ordination, is not just another work choice; it is rather an expression and confirmation of both service and commitment that reflects a particular identity. There can be no cessation of this reality upon retirement, and to reduce and minimize any personal crisis, the Church needs to give expression to the continuation of the priestly vocation and experience.

At a time when the issues of pension contributions and payments are part of the national debate and consideration, the Church should be at the forefront of ensuring generous and continued provision for those who have exercised a ministry of service and often sacrifice. If such requires the reduction of other expenditure, which could include episcopal expenditure, support for cathedrals, senior clergy, and administrative and central structures and institutions, then the Church should not be afraid to exercise a review of priorities. The matter and need for trade union recognition should also be considered in respect of terms and conditions, and pensions. With the elimination of freehold and the introduction of common tenure, such should be an obvious development given the current direction of an increased employment model in the Church.

The issue of ongoing pastoral and friendship relations from the retiring parish is problematic for the reasons already stated. Whether it is always desirable that priests should move from their previous parish and relationships should at the very least be a topic for discussion and consideration within the diocese. There is a real risk of retired isolation, which is clearly not a desirable outcome.

Finally, I would want to emphasize a matter concerning priesthood retirement which is unlikely to receive universal agreement. However, it is one personally felt and reflects a particular ecclesiology and theology of ordination and priesthood. It would be my contention that, just as the Church cannot be the Church without the celebration of the Eucharist, neither can a priest, being the minister/president of the Eucharist, be a priest without presiding at the Eucharist. In any retirement situation, and depending upon the particular outlook of the priest, the Church, through the diocese and possibly the deanery, should ensure that there are sufficient opportunities for the retired priest to preside at the Eucharist. The organization and arrangement of such should not be difficult, providing there is sufficient encouragement and recognition of the requirement.

Whether being a "substitute priest" is all-defining of the priestly vocation and experience is open to question. The need to ensure continued affirmation of identity and practice, within the limits of both health and age, should be the priority for a Church which professes care as a core principle. The retired priest is not a dinosaur from a previous era, but rather a person who often has still much to offer and to give. Being in retirement, as a priest, is not like being a member of a Darby and Joan Club (with no disrespect to this much-valued organization) that caters for a very different way of living subsequent to retirement; it is to be a living member of a living organism, namely the Church, which most retired clerics would wish to continue to serve. Perhaps a "House of Retired Priests" could be incorporated into the synodical structures that would enable a continued outward and visible sign of the inward and spiritual reality of ministerial priesthood. It is to be hoped that further consideration will be given to the role of the retired priest who will increasingly be called upon to serve God and God's people in the ongoing life of the Church.

8. MISSION, SPIRITUAL DIRECTION, AND RESEARCH

John Holmes

"You have been retired now for more than nine years, yet you still seem to be pretty active," a non-churchgoing friend said to me recently. "What do you do?" I paused for a moment to try to convey well the heart of what I do now as a retired Anglican priest. "I listen, I speak, I write," I said. That seemed a succinct summary of my ministry now in mentoring and spiritual direction, in preaching and teaching, and in writing and researching. But it was not like that when I first retired.

Then the first challenge was to find a house. Rosemary and I had married in 1965, halfway through my preparation for ordination at Lincoln Theological College. From that day until our retirement in 2007—we both retired at the same time—Rosemary and I had lived in a succession of rented properties and clergy houses. I was determined that our retirement home should be our own. I wanted my very creative and imaginative wife to bring to the house to which we retired her full repertoire of creative gifts.

While many clergy do not have the resources to fulfil such an ambition, we were fortunate. With the support of our three children and their partners and our own savings we were able to buy a three-bedroom semi-detached house in Whitkirk on the eastern edge of Leeds. The whole of our lives and ministry had been in Yorkshire, much of it in Leeds where I served as a parish priest for nearly twenty-seven years. After that I had been a diocesan missioner in the Diocese of Ripon (as it was then) living in North Yorkshire, and then canon missioner at Wakefield Cathedral serving the Diocese of Wakefield, back in West Yorkshire. Retiring to East Leeds, less than half a mile from junction 46 of the M1 motorway, seemed a good way to remain close to many friends and still be in good access for our own family.

BEGINNING RETIREMENT

We completed the purchase of our retirement home on Maundy Thursday in 2006, sixteen months before retiring. The house, built in 1937, needed substantial renovation, which made the purchase price accessible for us and also gave Rosemary scope to redesign it in a number of significant ways. After exhaustive work by others and ourselves, we moved in on 31 July 2007.

I began retirement on 1 August 2007 resolving to undertake no ministerial duties for six months on the advice of my spiritual director and other wise friends. So I did. My future ministry then was like a blank sheet of paper. The six-month break was good for both of us. We had been very active in Christian ministry for more than forty years. My wife had been a teacher and lecturer, and for a time children's work advisor in the Diocese of Ripon. We relished our new home and a good holiday and more space to catch up with family and friends. We had more time for our leisure pursuits, and we developed a keen interest in art history, attending lectures and making visits. This gave us more time to enjoy our marriage and our life together.

During the six-month break from active ministry, a friend had told me, the future shape of any retired ministry would begin to emerge. And so it did. Of course, there had always been invitations, to take the funeral of a friend or family member, or assist with former parishioners. I was invited, too, to be involved in weddings of family and friends. Local clergy asked me to assist with ministry on days off and holiday cover. I knew though that I wanted to do more than that. There were two reasons.

The first was vocational. Both as a parish priest and then a diocesan missioner, the centre of my ministry has always been a concern for mission and growth. It was Anglican ordinands at Leeds University, headed for the College of the Resurrection at Mirfield, who had shared their faith with me and encouraged me—still agnostic—to worship with them. I had been confirmed while away at boarding school. But the faith I encountered at university was much richer to my taste. Beautiful worship, a passion for social justice, and a strong desire to live and share the gospel. I started going to church again with new commitment in April 1962, and by the autumn I was enquiring about ordination.

I wanted to carry this concern for mission and growth into my retired ministry and not just into taking the occasional service. I had written about the joys and struggles of urban ministry in *When I am Weak* (Holmes, 1992). The book grew out of nearly fourteen years in the inner-city parish of St Luke's Beeston Hill (later renamed St Luke's Holbeck), where we saw considerable engagement with the needs of the local neighbourhood and significant growth in the size and commitment of the congregation. In 1999, I became a founder member of the Church of England's College of Evangelists, a fellowship of lay people, priests, bishops, and religious with a wide evangelistic ministry. As a diocesan missioner I wrote booklets about mission and growth. How could I carry those vocational concerns into my ministry as a retired priest?

Alongside this vocational concern there was also a financial one. Though much of the purchase price of our retirement house was paid on the day we bought it, I did take out a small interest-only mortgage which I needed to pay. Our church and state pensions were not sufficient to do this. I did need to generate a small additional income to do so.

ENGAGING IN MISSION

As I took up my ministry again after my six-month break, two opportunities presented themselves for me to pursue my concerns for mission and growth, and receive some remuneration in doing so. The first was a three-year commitment to support a local parish whose vicar was a long-time friend and former congregation member of mine. He had just been appointed rural dean of a large and demanding deanery on top of his considerable parish duties. He had been tasked with bringing two parishes together into one congregation in the larger and most significant of the church buildings. He had made great strides with that, but was eager after a period of parochial introspection to help turn the congregation outwards to the large and growing neighbourhood in a town in West Yorkshire.

The friend and I met and devised a plan for me to work one day a week and one Sunday a month as a "parallel church minister" with a modest reimbursement for my expenses and my time. The title of the post was his not mine. I would have preferred "parish missioner" or the like, but I did like the ministry opportunity being offered. Basically, my role was to contact those in touch with the church through baptisms, funerals, and weddings, seeking to serve them well and endeavouring to draw them into the church's worshipping life. I would be a member of the church's staff team (vicar, curate, parish administrator, and children centre staff) and work collaboratively with other congregation members in all we undertook. The project was approved by the parochial church council, who knew of me from my earlier work as diocesan missioner and a Holy Week programme to which I had contributed. The three years spent with the parish were a considerable help to the parish's mission and an enriching experience for my own ministry. The small regular additional income relieved any anxiety I had about the mortgage payments.

That opportunity was supplemented by occasional invitations to undertake mission consultancy in several dioceses across the country. These grew from working in earlier years as part of a national missioners network. These invitations usually consisted of conference work or smaller workshop-based days. There was always an agreed fee for these days with expenses.

Canon Robert Warren, who had been the national officer for evangelism for the Church of England from 1993–8 and had retired from stipendiary ministry a couple of years before me, has been a good companion and wise guide in my ministry in retirement. On my financial challenges he said, "In retirement, John, when responding to significant invitations from dioceses or large parishes, you need to be counterintuitive. Ask about the fee first." Robert had, like myself, usually raised the subject last with such requests, if at all. Spending considerable time in preparation and then presentation and interaction was always a joy to me, but a modest book token on one major diocesan occasion a long way from home didn't put much petrol in the tank or meet other expenses involved.

Clarifying the fee and expenses first saved embarrassment and I believe raised expectations too.

Such was the shape of my ministry as a retired priest in the first years after completing my nine years as canon missioner in the Diocese of Wakefield. From the end of 2007 to the spring of 2012, I was able to pursue my concerns of mission and growth for the wider Church.

In 2012, I was first asked to answer some statistical questions for some national government-funded research. The questions and several conversations that contained them over the next couple of years were about continuing to do some paid work while retired from my full-time paid occupation. We are a growing group within wider British society apparently.

I discovered, through answering the questions put to me, that for the years of my retirement from 2008 through to most of 2014 I was working between fifteen and twenty hours a week and on occasion more than that. Yet I rarely worked in the evening; my wife and I enjoyed much more good time together and with our growing family and did much walking and art exploration.

"I listen, I speak, I write." I had thus summarized my retired ministry to an enquiring friend. It was in the third of these actions my ministry was to develop significantly from the spring and summer of 2012.

ENGAGING IN RESEARCH

On 25 May 2012 a news item in the *Church Times* announced, "C of E to investigate how churches grow". The report went on to describe the launch of an eighteen-month Church Growth Research Programme. This was a joint initiative of the Archbishops' Council and the Church Commissioners. There were different strands to this research. There was to be a survey of 4,000 local churches led by Professor David Voas of the Institute of Economic and Social Studies at the University of Essex (see Voas & Watt, 2014). Other strands focused on particular aspects of church life known to be growing, such as church planting, fresh expressions, and (where I had special experience) cathedrals and greater parish churches. It was the cathedral strand of the research that I was invited to lead with a research assistant and under the overall direction of Dr David Goodhew of Cranmer Hall, St John's College, Durham.

This invitation and the challenging work involved came to me because of my years as a diocesan missioner in two dioceses, my continued involvement in mission and work on church growth since retiring from stipendiary ministry, and my experience of cathedral life and work with other cathedral staff across the country on issues of mission and growth.

It was, nonetheless, a daunting task. I had first to win the trust of cathedral deans to work with me on this research. I received great help from them, but initially some were suspicious, thinking this research would be used to cut central church support for cathedral life and work. I was also working alongside other researchers, some with a considerable list of academic qualifications. I received great help from David Goodhew, and my research assistant Ben Kautzer became an outstanding contributor to the work in his care over the statistics and his clarity of thinking and warm collaboration in the whole process of the research. He was appointed by David Goodhew and myself in July 2012 and worked with me on the research and production of the report which was presented, along with the other findings of the different strands, at a National Conference in London in January 2014 entitled *From Anecdote to Evidence* (Church of England, 2014). Our own findings were published in the report *Cathedrals, Greater Churches and the Growth of the Church* (Holmes & Kautzer, 2013).

I was expected to work on this research one full day a week for eighteen months and was reimbursed for doing so. In fact, the project took much more of my time than that. As well as a residential conference with other researchers and periodic day gatherings, I spent four full weeks visiting four cathedrals (Birmingham, Gloucester, Southwell, and Wakefield) and with Ben Kautzer's assistance surveyed worshippers (through a simple questionnaire) at sixty-one services, including all their Sunday services and most of their weekday services too. This element of the research became essential to explore beyond the statistics just why cathedrals were growing, not just in visitors but also crucially in worshippers. Who are those being added to cathedral congregations and why do they come? The worshipper surveys, as we called them, were crucial to the evidence-based nature of our research.

It was strange, shortly after my seventieth birthday, to begin this major new piece of work, researching and eventually writing too. My wife and I had celebrated my seventieth birthday in April 2012 by walking over four days St Cuthbert's Way from Melrose to Lindisfarne. She was always a stronger walker than me. Her support for my work on cathedrals research was equally important. She supported me in the decision to undertake it and helped me with it. She came with me to Gloucester Cathedral for the week's work there and also helped me type up the final report.

I soon found on beginning this research that I needed to say "no" to other requests for ministry, in particular preaching and taking services. Sundays I now spent worshipping with my wife at Wakefield Cathedral where we had returned after a gap on retiring. There had been no difficulty in going back to the cathedral. My wife was able to continue her active lay involvement there in a variety of ways, and I found myself joining the growing numbers of retired clergy, wives, and widows who find their way to cathedrals for worship these days.

After the cathedral research was completed, I was asked to follow it through in 2014. This involved speaking on the findings at meetings and conferences for cathedrals, greater churches with a cathedral-like ministry, and other groups with a concern for mission and growth.

SPIRITUAL DIRECTION AND MENTORING

There was one other sphere of ministry I undertook which had begun when I was a parish priest and developed more as a diocesan missioner. It is the ministry of spiritual director or companion. I enjoyed listening to those who sought my time and counsel. To clergy and to those in full-time lay ministry who came to see me at home I was happy to offer my time as a gift. I never saw regularly more than six people at any one time.

If the volume of work involved in the cathedral research precluded me offering much help for local churches and clergy, it did not prevent me from continuing my listening ministry with individuals, especially clergy. In fact, in 2012 this ministry had begun to become more focused. In particular, I was being asked to give support to two groups of clergy. First, there were experienced parish clergy with larger congregations and parishes and those too with diocesan responsibilities for mission and growth. Secondly, over recent years I have been giving support to less experienced clergy becoming incumbents for the first time or moving towards that responsibility.

This more focused work with individuals, more mentoring than spiritual companionship, grew out of some particular work I had been doing for a number of years with a large diocese in the Midlands on larger churches. Conference work led to more focused help with individual clergy. The diocese was introducing a Mission Action Planning programme, and I was one of a number of outside consultants asked to help with that. Initial phone contact with clergy discussing and reviewing their parishes' Mission Action Plans (often called MAPs) led in some instances to developing a relationship of support, with the diocese's permission. In 2010, I was asked, with others, to act as consultant for a small group of clergy of larger churches. We have met now for six years, twice a year for three hours, including a light lunch usually in a local public house. The clergy support one another, all serving large parishes with churches that have a strong eucharistic pattern of worship and many shared opportunities and challenges in public worship and ministry. I see some of the clergy individually at other times and facilitate their discussion when we meet together.

The work with less experienced clergy developed when I was asked to mentor four clergy undertaking new responsibilities. As I undertook this ministry rooted in the deep listening which is seen as fundamental to this work, I was reminded how fortunate I was to have had two curacies rather than the one considered sufficient these days. After serving my first three years in my title parish as curate, I was invited to consider a second curacy with a little more responsibility. I was pleased to consider this, but disappointed the greater responsibility was not a church as priest-in-charge. My spiritual director challenged me not to run before I could walk. "You have so many years of ministry ahead of you. Do not rush into responsibility. Use your second curacy to prepare yourself thoroughly for the greater responsibility coming your way in good time."

That memory came back to me as I listened to a young priest in his first incumbency. He had three suburban villages, each with its own church, close to a large city. He faced in his comparative inexperience big issues: the addition of another parish and church to the benefice; the bereavement faced by one village losing both vicar and vicarage; the different traditions of worship; and the spiritual needs of his own young family. I was pleased to serve him and see him move from uncertainty and anxiety to growing confidence and wisdom, and see the three churches begin to grow in confidence themselves, with one in particular encouraged by a good number of young families joining regularly in worship. Of course, others contributed to his encouraging story, but an experienced and supportive listening presence definitely made a real difference. Such stories are being told around the country as other retired clergy offer their support to others in positions of new, greater responsibility. Here surely is a resource which could and should be used more widely.

FACING BEREAVEMENT

"I listen, I speak, I write." But then on 23 December 2014 I stepped back from active ministry when we learnt Rosemary was suffering from terminal illness. The scans on 31 December showed the full extent of her lung cancer. My life and love and ministry became wholly focused on my wife in the final months of her life. She died on 2 April 2015, Maundy Thursday, in St Gemma's Hospice in Leeds. My involuntary sabbatical became intentional over the summer months that followed as I struggled with the reality of my loss. Rosemary and I had been partners in ministry as we were in love, marriage, and family life for fifty years.

I did continue a small amount of listening to individual clergy, those experienced and those much earlier on their ministry journeys. In the autumn, I took two short retreats to help discern my next steps. I decided to write a memoir of my wife's life for our eleven grandchildren. I wrote it in Lent 2016—it was very emotional to do so, but therapeutic and thoroughly worthwhile. It took several weeks to prepare it for publication, but on 12 September 2016 in Wakefield Cathedral I launched the publication of *A Beautiful Life* (Holmes, 2016) with my youngest son Tom, an actor, reading extracts to a large gathering of family, friends, and cathedral community. At the end of a successful evening which several grandchildren attended I felt a sense of relief but also of completion. Many have commented that my writing has captured the inspiration of Rosemary's life and faith.

I had begun to respond to speaking and preaching invitations. My spiritual director told me that my ministry would be different from now on. I will be less active. I am older and wiser and more prayerful, though still deeply flawed. But the inspiration remains the same as it has been for many years. With Timothy and all his physical and spiritual struggles, I still want to respond to the same call St Paul articulated: "As for you, always be sober, endure suffering, do the work of an evangelist, carry out your ministry fully" (2 Timothy 4:5).

REFERENCES

Church of England (2014), *From Anecdote to Evidence: Findings from the Church Growth Research Programme 2011–2013*, London: Archbishops' Council.

Holmes, J. (1992), *When I Am Weak*, London: Darton, Longman and Todd.

Holmes, J. (2016), *A Beautiful Life*, Lulu.

Holmes, J., & Kautzer, B. (2013), *Cathedrals, Greater Churches and the Growth of the Church (The Church Growth Research Programme: Report on Strand 3a)*, London: Church of England.

Voas, D., & Watt, L. (2014), *Numerical Change in Church Attendance: National, Local and Individual Factors (The Church Growth Research Programme: Report on Strands 1 and 2)*, London: Church of England.

9.   HOSPITAL CHAPLAINCY AND MENTORING

Tony Neal

I retired in the autumn of 2006, which was only slightly earlier than my sixty-fifth birthday, when I had originally planned to retire. My doctor had been worried about my health and had asked me more than once if I would be sensible and ask the Church for early retirement. Sadly I was not very sensible and dragged my feet over the matter, probably for a number of reasons, not least for what I thought was vocation, but also because, if I am honest, I had founded my team ministry, and I probably thought they could not do without me. A decent early retirement would have been perhaps four years before the usual age, but I eventually opted for four months—not the best result as history will show.

FINDING A HOME FOR RETIREMENT

My wife and I did not have enough money of our own to buy a house, so we applied for, and were granted, a Church of England Pensions Board house. The process for finding a house could only begin in the final six months of working life and the first step was to look at a very long list of houses from all over the country, none of which were in Cornwall, where I had been serving for most of my ministry; so we rejected the list. In the circumstances, we had to look for a house in Cornwall on behalf of the Board. We were told that the only price the Board could afford was £150,000, although they were prepared to look at a slightly more expensive house if the Diocese of Truro was prepared to help with some more money. Sadly, the diocese was not prepared to help, even though they would have had the money returned, as with any investment, with a good profit. The sort of money we were talking about was £20,000 at the most, and it would have made, in those days, the purchase of a bungalow a lot more possible for retirement.

We found a house in Camborne, a former industrial town where there was a lot of nineteenth-century housing, and which was close to where two of our children lived then. Living close to children is very important for many reasons to most families, but it is not always possible to live close to them all, and in our case our other two children were living and working in London.

The house was approved by the Board's surveyor, who also suggested there should be central heating and some other small additions which were paid for by the Board. There is no garden at the front of the house, but much to our delight there is a long garden at the rear which covers one of our hobbies. We are situated in the centre of Camborne and close to the bus and train stations, and to the major shops, doctors, and dentists, as well as restaurants and churches. The area is quiet, and the neighbours are very pleasant. The only problem is that our road is accessible to visitors to Camborne, giving them free parking which often obstructs the residents. How nice it was to be spoilt once and have a rectory with its own drive and garage.

Our rent is deducted at source and changes from year to year and at the time we began our tenancy was 30 per cent of my church pension plus 3 per cent from other sources. As the pension went up year-by-year so would our rent and here it often exceeded what other residents paid. That is a changing situation. Our rent is now coming down to be in line with average local rent and there may be other deductions. It was the case that we were paying rent that was more acceptable in a wealthier area.

BEGINNING RETIREMENT

Our official retirement was in September 2006, but it was not possible to move until March 2007 because the previous owner of the house had problems over a divorce, and there was lack of agreement between the couple. Once agreement between them was in place, our house could be paid for and the alterations carried out. Then, in March 2007, we moved in and began a very happy time in residence, however much we sometimes moan about the landlord. At my request the bishop came and blessed the house, which was uplifting for us.

In the Truro Diocese, it is normal for retired clergy not to undertake any locum work for the first six months of retirement, thus no permission to officiate (PTO) is issued until later. At this stage, my wife continued to worship at one of my former churches where my daughter also worshipped, and as she lived close to Camborne, she was able to give my wife a lift. My wife kept her involvement purely to worship and nothing else, but it did mean she was still able to see friends, and that is important for a clergy wife. Why should a woman (or in our own times a man) be punished for being married to a priest?

On the other hand, it is right that a parish priest has only a slender connection with his or her former parishes, and when he or she does the present incumbent must give permission. I had already arranged to worship some twelve miles from Camborne in St Agnes on the North Coast, where a young man who had been a former parishioner of mine was the incumbent. He had two churches, so three services were held on a Sunday morning. The vicar had no curate at the time, so he was glad to see retired clergy. Once I got my PTO I was happy to assist on a Sunday morning. Then in the week there were two Eucharists and the inevitable weddings and funerals. The vicar was also the rural dean, so he would sometimes ask us retired clergy to go to help in parishes that had an interregnum. So there was plenty to keep me interested in those early days after the PTO was issued. There were also opportunities for pastoral care and for ensuring that the liturgical seasons were kept as they should be. The vicar was on the ball and the growth of his congregation reflected his ability as a priest. He was energetic, popular, and a good pastor and administrator, but he was not beyond asking for advice if he felt he needed it. It was no surprise when the vicar became a non-residentiary canon and when he followed in my footsteps as chair of the House of Clergy.

One interesting sideline in the early years of my retirement was that Methodists began to ask me to conduct worship if I was free, and I was very glad to accept such invitations. I was usually asked by a minister I knew, but sometimes it was someone who had heard that I was supportive of the Anglican and Methodist relationship. From the time when I first arrived in Cornwall, I had been able to form good relationships with Methodist ministers, and then the relationship grew out to our congregations. Indeed, within the team ministry of which I was the rector, in the small country parish of Gwinear, we signed a joint Anglican Methodist Covenant, which effectively brought us together in every respect. I have taken every opportunity I can to encourage more use being made of the Covenant.

There was once an awful time in Cornwall where relationships between Anglicans and Methodists were dire, but that is very much history now. In fact, ecumenical relationships in Cornwall are very good indeed, and it is quite possible to expect unity between Anglicans and Methodists, and we pray for that. Unity with the Roman Catholics may take longer, but there are some good signs which give hope. Like the Methodist chair of district, the Roman Catholic bishop is an honorary canon of Truro Cathedral.

I ought to mention that, while I was still in the parish of St Agnes that I joined on retirement in 2006, besides the Methodists requesting me to conduct worship I also had requests from Anglicans, but usually from only those who were in the deanery of my vicar, who was their rural dean. Another high point of my time at St Agnes was in 2009, when they allowed me to celebrate my fortieth anniversary of ordination to the priesthood in their church on the Feast of Saint Matthew with a sung Eucharist. The vicar was the preacher.

During my time at St Agnes I had also decided to study, through research, for a Master of Philosophy degree awarded by Glyndŵr University and the University of Wales. The degree was gained by research on a lay training project in the Diocese of Truro called "The People of God Initiative" (Neal, 2012). It was a very interesting subject that was important to the diocese and its future development. I got very stimulated by research, wished I had discovered it much sooner, and have gone on subsequently with other projects.

EXPLORING HOSPITAL CHAPLAINCY

After a couple of years with St Agnes I was approached by my first curate, who was at the time senior chaplain at Treliske Hospital in Truro, and he asked me if I would be willing to help out in the chaplaincy. I had been a chaplain in a small hospital in my first parish in West Cornwall and also a hospice which was in the hospital grounds; both were run by Roman Catholic nuns, but nothing like as big as Treliske. The senior chaplain had always wanted to work in chaplaincy, and I had encouraged him to do so, because he showed me through the work he did in our hospital and hospice how suited he was for it. I therefore felt I needed to do something to help him out at Treliske as he had too few staff. However, I said I would have to limit myself to two days a week, and not on Sundays, as I was both retired and helping at St Agnes. He agreed and I was paid by the NHS, but some weeks I might not be paid at all if infection broke out and my presence was not wanted. I did not let the hospital affect what I did at St Agnes, but the two jobs together were equal to four days a week. Now I wonder how wise that may have been, but I never used to think like that as my GP knew. Vocation first and health second.

I believe that one of our most important jobs was to care for the staff as well as for the patients, and some of us tried to do that. However, there was no training for us in what in other places could be known as industrial chaplaincy, so how could we really understand the jobs of others? Moreover, quite a lot of the varied staff did not really understand the job of chaplains, so I could see that there was real opportunity for collaboration and education across the other roles with which we work. Indeed, some fellow workers in hospital do not approve of money being spent on chaplaincy and believe the money would be better spent on medical professionals, drugs, or equipment.

One thing with which I could not come to terms was what I saw as one long dash around the hospital, when it would have been a delight to sit with patients for longer and likewise with fellow members of staff.

When the chaplain returned to the office it would be part of every day to fill in forms to report the numbers of contacts made, and "one" or "two" would not be a good commendation of the chaplaincy.

One important point that was often overlooked was that people stayed for a shorter time in hospital with the advance in medical science and the majority were discharged by the weekend. However, the more seriously ill were kept in at weekends, and they were not able to cope with leaving their ward for the chapel. This meant that smaller numbers came to chapel, but more were ministered to on their wards. Some people could not understand this and would criticize us for not getting people to chapel on a Sunday.

Although most of the patients are present during the week, it was just not possible to minister to all of them successfully, because they were so hard to meet, and patients were not always allowed off a ward for a service in the chapel as their treatment was a priority. There are a number of issues here that hospital management would be wise to discuss with chaplains to the benefit of everyone.

However, as I spent time in the hospital, I realized just how large it really was. Working in an institution of that size did not suit me at all; indeed, I have been in parishes with fewer parishioners. There were smaller hospitals throughout Cornwall that were added to the chaplaincy such as in Penzance, Hayle, Redruth, St Austell, and Newquay, to which all chaplains had to take a share on a rota. Once, all the small hospitals would have had a local parish priest as chaplain who would be easier to contact and more able to attend the hospital quickly in an emergency. I know that from my own experience.

It was always a joy to go to one of the smaller hospitals from my point of view, and I very much liked Hayle Hospital and the Marie Therese Treatment Centre for people with physical disability; both could be dealt with in half a day. We were sometimes asked to conduct funerals, and I remember an elderly lady in Treliske who had no relatives at all. It was more usual for chaplains to conduct the blessing, or baptism, of stillborn babies than to conduct their funerals. Showing the love of God to these children, and their parents, overcomes harsh doctrine on baptism. Living children who are baptized at birth are sad enough but mostly survive, but the stillborn are a tragedy for parents and they call a lot of love out of us—that is a privilege for priests and one of the things that makes ministry worthwhile.

On the other hand, a wedding is a happy occasion and two of us were privileged to conduct the wedding of a young lady who had been detained in hospital for a significant period. Her family and children were present with a good number of nurses and doctors, and it was more like being in a parish church.

One other good pastoral experience was on an isolation ward which was physically separated from the main body of the hospital and was purely for those who had serious infections. Most of the patients were in single rooms which had doors and could not be entered without gowns and masks. Most of the patients were kept on the unit for something like three months to recover, and it was a difficult time for patients and staff. However, I found it was a happy environment for me as I could spend more time with the patients and staff there, unlike the rest of the hospital. As patients did not see many visitors, they were often glad to see me for some conversation. I also trained for feeding patients at lunch time on the unit, so that was one way to help the staff and get to know the patients better from my point of view, using my time in the hospital more fully.

In the chapel area, there was a room for the Muslim patients to pray, and since I was there, the area has improved, so that they can wash as well. Most of the Muslims seemed to be doctors, but there were others, and they were all impressive in their witness to their faith. The chapel was there for all denominations, and none, and a number of people came in every day to sit and be quiet, or welcome having support from a chaplain. We had a long list of Christian priests and ministers, and ministers of other faiths, who could be contacted if a patient contacted us. We even had the name of a witch.

BECOMING A MENTOR

During 2010, I had been involved on a Sunday with some parishes at the request of my vicar, who was also the rural dean and therefore keeping his eye on those parishes where there was a vacancy for an incumbent; sadly they were not happy places. One place that I visited worried me a great deal as the congregation was split right down the middle and not frightened of open warfare. I clearly remember driving home and thinking how glad I was that I would never have to go back to that parish ever again. That was the wrong conclusion and instead of putting the issue out of my mind, it remained firmly in it, and the reason for that was that I realized I had the experience to help that parish and that God might be challenging me to use that experience. It was also the case that I was not as at home in chaplaincy as in parish ministry. I decided that I needed to go to see the bishop, and I did.

The bishop had no problem with offering me a job working with a man who was going to care for seven parishes and eight churches. I had told the bishop about my feelings for the parish I had visited and that it was very much in my mind, and amazingly that parish was one of the ones they were planning to put together. Everything was falling into place, and that was further strengthened by my meeting with the proposed incumbent; he had no problem in accepting me.

I took to the new incumbent immediately in the meetings we had, and it was quite clear that he was more than willing to admit he had no experience of running a parish, and certainly not a team of seven parishes, and to welcome calling on my expertise. His experience of ordained ministry had been as a self-supporting minister (SSM). Professionally he was a dentist, with a professional doctorate, who had taught in a dental school, practised in a community practice, and worked as an NHS executive. He had been a priest for less than ten years.

We had a lot of conversation to begin with as we needed to sort everything out and make our views and opinions clear so we could avoid problems later. We were aware that we were from different traditions in the Church, in that he was an Evangelical and I am a Liberal Catholic. But we were able, while respecting each other's points of view, to support team ministry and collaborative ministry. We both valued mentoring as well, and in his professional life mentoring was common practice in the NHS.

The bishop had no problem with the new incumbent and me being in a relationship of mentor and mentee, but I would also be an associate priest working on a half-time basis, so I would not be a parochial supervisor. It is the incumbent that is being mentored, but he is in charge of the parish. Mentoring an incumbent is quite different from mentoring a curate who is in a junior role. A mentor is an advisor, or guide, not someone with power; so if the mentor's advice is rejected that is how it has to be. If the relationship has been talked about sensibly and frankly from the beginning, there should be few problems later.

The bishop did invite me to work full-time, and to be paid a full-time stipend, but I asked instead to be part-time and have a part-time stipend. The bishop was happy to accept that, and I had to remember that I was retired, needed relaxation, and should keep an eye on my health. As regards being paid, it was not as wonderful as it sounded. I had a pension from the Church, a pension from my teaching job in the 1970s, the state pension, and now half a stipend; but, of course, that meant I now paid more rent to the Church of England and more tax to the government. So I considered it better to reject mammon in favour of job satisfaction, which I certainly had.

The new incumbent and I were given separate interviews by a representative body of lay people from the seven parishes, and we were found fit for office. I started work almost immediately in September 2010, but the incumbent had to wait until January 2011, as he had to work out his notice to the NHS.

When the incumbent arrived, we had a service led by the bishop to inaugurate what became known as the Cluster, and that was followed by every church having a welcome Eucharist for the new incumbent at which either he preached or I did, and the other one celebrated. Then it was full steam ahead. I had two parishes for which I was particularly responsible, but that did not mean I never went anywhere else, as we were low on clergy to begin with. We had a Cluster meeting every week on a Thursday, when the clergy and those readers who were available met around a Eucharist. This was a focal point of our life together and was not to be missed. Gradually we became deep in friendship and shared ministry.

As a mentor over the three years or so that I worked in what we called the Eight Saints Cluster, I shared with the incumbent and other colleagues what mentoring was not about. I have actually referred to one point already, namely that mentoring an incumbent is quite different from mentoring a curate because the incumbent may need help, but he is in charge of the Cluster, so the mentor is not a supervisor. A mentor is certainly not a substitute parent and should not encourage an incumbent to become dependent. The mentor should not be a problem solver, or someone who has all the answers. The mentor should certainly not be someone who mentions his own parishes and how wonderful they were.

I felt I could never be judge and jury over the performance of the incumbent, because that would only have made me an intimidating presence to the mentee, and our relationship would have crashed. Likewise, it would have been unwise for a mentor to report on the incumbent's progress, or lack of it, to a bishop or an archdeacon behind the incumbent's back. If a report is ever to be made, it should be transparent and in collaboration between mentor and mentee, because such a relationship is only going to flourish if trust is paramount. At the beginning of the relationship full discussion must be held so that the mentor and incumbent are quite clear what their expectations of the mentoring relationship are. Getting to know each other is crucial. It would be better that a couple parted amicably at the beginning than go forward to damaging problems. One thing that should be discussed at the beginning is to ask what the incumbent actually learnt in his or her curacy, especially if they served as an SSM. For example, what experience have they really had conducting weddings and funerals. Honesty at this stage will avoid what could be embarrassing mistakes later. Filling in the gaps of an incumbent's experience is essential because, once inducted, an incumbent is going to be pushed in at the deep end.

Likewise, a discussion should be had about churchmanship. In our case, we had an Evangelical incumbent and one Anglo-Catholic parish that had signed Resolutions A and B and was against women priests, while the remaining parishes were Liberal Catholic. The main service in all of them was the Eucharist. The new incumbent was very flexible and was willing to learn how to celebrate the services in his new Cluster in ways that respected their traditions. I was able to help teach what the new man needed to know, but he was also very good at watching what the rest of us did. I made a point to encourage parishioners to respect the tradition of the incumbent. It was good for us that we learnt a lot from the incumbent's tradition as he quietly showed us the benefits of non-eucharistic worship, and introduced us to different ways of prayer,

Bible study, and preaching. If we expect priests from a different tradition to respect our traditions, the least we can do is to respect theirs.

An important point for me to bear in mind was that I needed to be a listener and try to create a safe place of reflection and growth for the new incumbent, in the knowledge that the meetings between us were confidential. Contrary to what might happen for some mentors, I was actually in the Cluster Ministry Team, so it was important that I kept complete confidentiality at the same time as playing a full part in the life of the Cluster.

From the beginning of any situation like this there will be issues that present themselves for the new priest of which he or she will have no previous experience. It is for the incumbent to ask the mentor for help according to current needs. It did not seem to me a good idea to ask the incumbent if he needed any help, or advice, just because I felt like fulfilling my mentoring role. By working part-time in the Cluster I was able to fulfil another role, which was to mentor through example, because there were some matters that I could deal with on the incumbent's behalf, freeing him but at the same time ensuring the incumbent was involved in the process and able to learn from it. An example of that in more than one parish concerned the graveyards: in one parish extending the graveyard, in a second parish gaining a new graveyard, and in another parish sadly closing one. I could lay out to the incumbent what needed to be done, and the graveyard law, and discuss it with him for his future use. I would also report back when I had done something, which was a practical way of showing the incumbent what needed to be done. This was valuable at a time when the incumbent was under pressure, when so much needed to be done, at a time when eight churches had so many practical problems. As mentor, I could give practical help and then turn it into tuition.

Obviously, there were a number of matters that came up that were purely answered by discussion or advice such as the Worship Measure, ecumenism, training curates, PCC meetings, celebrating the seasons, divorce, and much more than can be listed here now. The three years I spent as a mentor were some of the happiest years of my ministry, and the incumbent was a delight to work with, as indeed were his colleagues both lay and ordained.

FACING ILLNESS

Looking back over the years of my retirement, I recognize that I had eight years of reasonable health, until 2015. In fact, the whole of 2015 was filled with illness, starting with a flare up of a family disease called Charcot Marie Tooth Disease, and just when I was getting over it, I had a haemorrhagic stroke. I am glad to say that Truro Hospital provides an excellent service, as does my Camborne GP, and they have helped me to healing, backed up by my wife, and powered by our Lord.

Back at the beginning of this century my then GP was worried about my health. She thought I was doing too much and ought to retire, which was a wise position, to which I ought to have given much more thought. If I had given more thought to that advice, perhaps I might not have had that subsequent period of illness; but I have now given a great deal of thought to the illness and begun to change my way of life.

My priority now is to my family and my home life, followed by a limited ministry. I have accepted that my age and my post-illness condition, while improving, will not now allow me to drive, but they will allow me to follow theology and prayer, and to do some gardening. I also gave thought to some words a priest gave me when he was concerned at the amount of work I was doing. Quite simply he said, "Relax, you have done everything you ever needed to do, so let go." I can honestly see the sense of that now.

REFERENCE

Neal, A. T. (2012), The People of God Initiative: Evaluating a lay training programme in the Diocese of Truro 2001–2010. Unpublished MPhil dissertation, Glyndŵr University.

10. MISSION PARTNERS AND THE RETIRED CLERGY ASSOCIATION

David Phypers

In 1985, I retired from school teaching on health grounds. I had been ordained six years previously and had been helping as a Non Stipendiary Minister (NSM) in an inner-suburban church in Derby. Three years after retirement I was offered a stipendiary post as priest-in-charge of two village parishes. At that point, with hindsight, we made our first mistake. Not wanting to be troubled with ongoing repairs and possible problems with tenants, we sold our house.

SETTLING INTO RETIREMENT AND PAYING THE RENT

We had been told that the Pensions Board would provide low-cost housing in retirement, would not charge more than 25 per cent of our pension in rent, and would continue to pay our water charges. That was not strictly true. We should have been told that the Board would charge up to 25 per cent of our joint gross income in rent. By the time I retired from stipendiary ministry in 2007, the 25 per cent had become 30 per cent, and we had to pay our water charges as well. These payments, along with Council Tax (which we had not paid when we lived in vicarages) amounted to 50 per cent of our net income. Our first month's rent, in a modest three-bedroom CHARM (Church's Housing Assistance for the Retired Ministry) house, was nearly £700. This increased year-by-year, until we were paying nearly £800 each month. Then, one day, out of the blue, we received a letter from the Pensions Board, saying that we had been overcharged, our rent was being reduced to £670 each month, and we would receive a £3,000 refund.

In 2015, the Pensions Board changed the way it calculates rents from the previous income-based formula to one based on the principle of "target rents" (supposedly about 60 per cent of market rents). When it then discovered we were paying £80 more each month than the market rent for our house, we received a further reduction. Under the current transitional arrangements, our rent will now reduce by £5 per month per annum for the next thirty years, until we should then be paying our correct target rent. I doubt we shall be around to reach this goal. Although the Pensions Board is an excellent landlord in maintaining our property, I am not the only retired clergyperson to be cynical about its "generosity" in providing housing in retirement. My cynicism is not helped by the Pensions Board's failure to itemize to its tenants its calculations in arriving at the target rents it now charges.

We served our last seven years of stipendiary ministry looking after four villages near Buxton and then returned to Derby to retire. A friend who is chairman of Derby Chamber Music Society told me of the imminent resignation of the society's treasurer. I had always refused to take on treasurer's work, saying I found it difficult to manage my own financial affairs, let alone the affairs of others. However, I agreed to become the new treasurer, and this, if you like, became my first area of retirement work. I enrolled for a local authority course in bookkeeping and found my treasurer's work expanding. I am now also treasurer of Workplace Chaplaincy in Derbyshire (formerly Industrial Mission in Derbyshire) and of the Retired Clergy Association of the Church of England. The chaplaincy work keeps me in touch with developments in the diocese and the national chaplaincy community.

In our final parish, we began to support two CMS Mission Partners and so started to receive regular newsletters and emails from CMS. From this I learned of a sponsored trek in the foothills of the Himalayas to take place four months into my retirement. Ten days in Nepal in the shadow of Annapurna in January 2008 was a never-to-be-forgotten experience. Besides the trek itself, we met Christian leaders in the country, saw something of the vitality of the Nepali church and, after the trek had finished, joined CMS partners from across India and South Asia who were meeting in conference together. After returning home I made a PowerPoint presentation of the trip and took it round various clubs and societies, raising further funds for CMS.

On my retirement, we returned to Derby and started to worship at a city-centre church. We knew the vicar, although by the time we arrived he had just moved to another living, so the parish was in vacancy. Nevertheless, the church was being ably led by an associate minister, and we settled in happily. Although at the time permission to officiate (PTO) was granted automatically in the Diocese of Derby to retiring clergy, we did nothing for six months. Then, as the vacancy was extended, my wife (who is a reader) and I began to take our turns in leading ministry. Together with another reader we ran an Alpha course and followed it up with a post-Alpha course on Sunday evenings. We followed Nicky Gumbel's *Searching Issues*, inviting specialist speakers to address the various topics: Derby Cathedral's then dean on science and faith; a minister/doctor on healing; a university chaplain on other faiths; and so on.

Now, under the new vicar, occasionally we both lead and preach. My wife has responsibility for a monthly midweek tea for older people, after which she leads evening prayer. I have become active with a reader and a Free Church minister in leading a midweek lunchtime service which attracts Christians and others from across Derby. Some of the many homeless people in the city sometimes join us, particularly for the free lunch which follows.

RETIRED CLERGY ASSOCIATION

When I retired, the Bishop of Derby offered to pay my lifetime subscription to the Retired Clergy Association (RCA), as he does to all retiring clergy. I knew nothing about RCA, but I gladly accepted. Because of my concerns about housing I began to attend the Association's general meetings each year. After two or three years, John Sansom, then secretary and treasurer, announced his desire to step down, so I wrote to ask him what was involved. He sent me an application form, so we met, along with

Bishop Richard Lewis, the then chair, and within three to four months, I became the new secretary and treasurer.

This work has given me a new lease of life. Despite what I was doing (and still am) I had become somewhat listless and bored. Suddenly I found new direction and purpose. Within eighteen months, Bishop Richard himself retired from the chair, and I began to form a new partnership with the new chair, Bishop David Jennings, retired Bishop of Warrington.

Along with the day-to-day work of admitting new members and maintaining the database (we have about 3,500 members), I produce and distribute three newsletters each year, prepare for and service twice-yearly council meetings, and similarly organize two general meetings. We hold one in the southern Province, and the other at Bishopthorpe, near York, where Archbishop John Sentamu is always our generous and gracious host.

My time with RCA has coincided with changes to the CHARM rental scheme referred to earlier. This has involved meetings with senior officials at the Pensions Board, as we have been consulted about the changes as they have proceeded. RCA has also been consulted about retired clergy conditions of service and about the deployment of retired clergy. These consultations have involved further meetings at Church House in London.

Interestingly, the RCA work is not just administrative. Sometimes, members get in touch about personal issues as well. Sometimes, though not always, these concern housing, and sometimes, because I know who to contact at the Pensions Board, these can be resolved. "I've never complained before, in my life," wept one member down the phone after everything that could have gone wrong had gone wrong with a double-glazing installation. Within a few weeks, the double-glazing was reinstalled, and the tenant was enjoying the protection from draughts and cold she rightly deserved.

Sadly, not all issues can be resolved so happily. I have also sat with a retired colleague and his wife who wept because they just cannot afford basic household expenses and their CHARM rent month-by-month without dipping into the lump sum that came with their pension. All I could say to them was that this is what they will have to do until their capital assets fall to £15,000 when they will begin to become eligible for pension benefits, which will then hopefully bridge the gap. Yes, the Pensions Board has appointed a Welfare Benefits Adviser to help in these situations, and she does. But is not the very fact of her appointment an indictment of a Church which still fails to provide adequate financial support in retirement for some of its clergy who have given a lifetime of sacrificial service?

None of this is the fault of Pensions Board officials themselves, who are Christian women and men of faith, compassion, and the highest integrity. But they work within a civil service mindset which sometimes makes them come across as cold and unfeeling. They also work within financial constraints imposed from the Archbishops' Council and the Church Commissioners, and this where the real faults lie.

CONTINUING MINISTRY

Retirement, for clergy, as for many other professionals, is not always easy. Many of us look forward to continuing ministry in one form or another, at least for a while. And some of us find that ministry in highly satisfying contexts. One of our members, who comes to our annual meetings, is still active in house-for-duty ministry well into his eighties. "They've told me they won't replace me," he says, "so I'm staying for as long as I can."

Others develop what I might call a "vacancy ministry". There are always parishes in vacancy, and when one vacancy ends in one place another one begins elsewhere. Along with ministry in my own church, I have developed fruitful relationships with different parishes during vacancies in the Diocese of Derby. I do not minister every week, but perhaps once every month or two as loyal churchwardens fill their pulpits and altars from available licensed clergy.

Two to three years before I retired from stipendiary ministry, I was invited by my diocese to attend a pre-retirement course. One of the contributors talked to us about spirituality and worship in retirement. "Choose your parish before you choose where to live," he advised, "and talk to the vicar beforehand to be sure he will be happy for you to join his congregation, and, if you wish, to continue in active ministry." Fine. But what do you do when a new vicar arrives and makes it clear that he/she does not want you anymore? We sat with just such a couple in another part of the country last year. Husband ordained and wife a reader, they had seen congregations grow during their "working" lives. They had settled happily into a new parish in retirement where they continued to be used in ministry in different ways. They still felt they had much to offer. Then came a new vicar who simply stopped asking them to assist, and who brought in fresh assistants of her own. They agreed they were perceived as a threat.

When we retire, we are no longer in control. Many of us find this very hard, because we have been in control in our ministry. Indeed, we have had to be. But now, when it comes to church life we are not. Closely allied to this, we also discover that what we have done previously counts for little, if at all. So, if we start to offer "advice" or, more seriously, criticism, without being asked, we shall quickly be seen as interfering, and as a possible nuisance.

THE GRACE OF HUMILITY

Many of today's clergy are seriously insecure. Indeed, with declining and aging congregations, this goes with the territory. The presence of a retired clergyperson in one of their congregations, particularly if that person has enjoyed a distinguished and "successful" ministry, may not be seen as an asset, but as a distinct disadvantage. Maybe, the retired minister might enjoy an invaluable role as a mentor to his or her younger colleague, or to an incumbent in another place, but that can only be by invitation. We have to learn again the grace of humility, and that is never easy. We have to bite our lips when we see the vicar making obvious mistakes. Often, all we can do is to pray, and to encourage others to pray if they come to us as ministers and grumble.

Sometimes, retired clergy are their own worst enemies. Years ago, a close colleague arrived in his parishes to find a retired priest virtually in charge in one of his churches. From day one he systematically undermined the new incumbent. "We will have a proper sermon tonight," he began, one evening, as he mounted the pulpit steps. Eventually, the bishop attended a PCC and declared the retired man *persona non grata* in the parish.

More recently, I have learned of two parishes in my own diocese where an incumbent has retired within his former benefice (surely, that should be preventable in some way) and has continued to behave as if he was still the vicar. In each case, the archdeacon has had formally to exclude that person from entering the church. In each case, the new incumbent was a woman.

Last year, I learned of a retired clergywoman who had ably guided her parish through a vacancy. She was then incensed to learn she would have no part to play, nor even be consulted, in the process of making the new appointment. But why should she be? When the new vicar arrives, her work in that parish, for the time being, will be done, and she should be glad to take a rest. With grace and humility, she may have a continuing ministry in that place, or she may need to be deployed elsewhere, or she may need to give up active "up front" ministry entirely. We must all do that, eventually, and we must be constantly alert to declining vigour and ability which, in time, will come to us all.

When I retired nine years ago, I never expected to become treasurer to three different organizations, nor to assume administrative responsibility with a national association. I am seeing retired clergy blossom as writers, or in overseas ministry, for example, which they had never enjoyed before. Others are finding new vocation in chaplaincy and counselling. We do not have to stay in parish ministry which, in itself, is changing rapidly.

Retirement can be fun. Do not let us spoil it for a new generation of younger clergy who have new vision and new purpose which they will pursue for the glory of God.

11.   FINDING A HOME AND MAKING A LIFE

Tim Newcombe

To mangle and misquote Jane Austen, it is a truth universally acknowledged that a single man, in want of a large fortune and only twenty years into a near forty-year stint in the stipendiary ministry of the Church of England, will not want to consider retirement. Neither will he want to think about the accommodation he may then need.

Fortunately for me, just at that time I was nagged about both of these matters by a very wise and persistent layman and his wife in the parish of which I was then the incumbent. The layman concerned kept pointing out to me that his grandfather had been a priest and had made provision for retirement. If I could but bring myself to think things through *and take action* in a timely fashion, I might end up owning a home of my own by the time I wanted to retire, rather than end up in a mess.

FINDING A HOUSE

Eventually, I was persuaded to find out just what mortgage I could have and how much I would have to repay each month. With that knowledge, the layman then challenged me to consider where I wanted to look for a property. He next took me to a nearby town of my choice, and as I looked into the estate agents' windows, he pointed out that I would never make any progress if I did not go in and get the details of affordable properties on the market. I have never felt more nervous or unskilled. Armed with the details, he then drove me around the town to look at the houses. Some I immediately discounted, and what I wanted and what I could buy for "my" money gradually became clearer. I was next advised by the same person to ask to see inside some of the properties. I was first tutored on how to view and how to be appreciative toward vendors without giving away anything that might lead me to paying more than I needed to later on.

On the way home, after an afternoon of viewings, I was comparing the houses and what each offered. In the course of conversation this layman turned to me and said, "You've made your choice already." He then pointed out that I was in fact comparing every house I had entered with one particular property. It was on that basis that I had a second viewing of that vacant house and then made an offer for it. I was not in a chain and neither were the vendors who had inherited the property on which a mortgage had been taken out. A prompt sale was sought, and I managed to purchase it for less than the asking price.

So twelve years before retiring I was the proud owner of a two up, two down, late-Victorian, end-of-terrace cottage with an integral bathroom, a bolt-on kitchen with a flat roof, off-street parking, and a "courtyard garden" (aka a backyard). Much needed to be done to the house, and some of the work was required as a condition of securing the mortgage. Other work was necessary to meet my immediate needs. Thanks to local contacts I found a good contractor who did the work promptly and to a high standard.

When some years later I was left a small inheritance, I was able to clear the mortgage and put further works in hand. This should mean that maintenance bills in the years ahead will be further reduced. Some three years after purchasing the house, I moved and took a parish about 135 miles from it. Rather than let it or sell it, I decided to keep it, continue renovating it and use it as a bolt hole for days off and holidays.

About three years before retiring, I began to wonder where I really would settle when I did retire. The Church of England Pensions Board at that time kept extending the period of service required to receive a full pension, but when the calculations were done, I decided that after thirty-seven years full-time stipendiary service I would go. I had seen numbers of parishioners over the years fail to reach retirement at all or get there and fall seriously ill and then never enjoy any quality of life in retirement. Staying for three or four more years to get the maximum lump sum and £200 more per annum was just too risky. I decided to embark on life in the army—the army of the retired. But where to live?

My siblings were fifteen and thirteen years my senior and one had already died. Their children, my nephews and nieces, were all adult and married. Now in their forties and fifties some had adult children of their own. They are scattered across southern England, with the exception of one who lives in the Far East. Though we all get on, I did not want to move to be near them and I certainly did not want to try and impose myself on any of them. I decided to retain the property and by about six months before retiring the house was just as I wanted it.

MAKING A HOME AND SETTLING IN

From all the furniture I had gained over the years to fill a standard sized parsonage, I selected the pieces I loved most; those that would fit in the space available and still allow me room to move around. Three months before retirement several large bits and pieces were sent to a sale room. Of the rest, items were either earmarked for an auction organized by the church (it raised £1,700 for church funds) or subsequently cleared away by the furniture removers.

Five days after a glorious final service with a congregation that included people from the five parishes in which I had served either as a curate or as an incumbent and the one in which I had grown up, my furniture, books, and fittings were out of the vicarage and into my new home. The vicarage was cleared and cleaned throughout and the keys handed back to the diocesan office. I understand that the following day the estate agent's board went up and within a week the vicarage had been let for six months. There was to be no going back. Though I had always accepted the wisdom of the convention that clergy should not retire into or near their old parishes, I was about to find out just how costly that convention really is.

It took a little while to bring order out of chaos, but within two or three weeks I had everything in place. Then the trouble began. I well remember sitting and looking around myself, gazing for some time at a picture and thinking, "What now? Will it be like this from now on?" I had moved into a small former market town set in many square miles of mixed farms and moorland. Though I knew where all the shops and facilities were, I knew nothing about the life of the community. I had also moved into a diocese in which I had never served and where I knew no one. My licence had gone. I was now a sixty-five-year-old single man who may have had an interesting ministerial life, but who now had to carve out a future. This change was much, much more than just a move; it was something completely new and required a reorientation that would demand engagement of heart, mind, and body. A day-long diocesan pre-retirement course had been helpful, but much of the time had been given over to housing and finance. The deeper issues had been ignored or skated over in that polite way that the Church of England does so well. It has to be said that, even if such things had been dealt with in greater depth, it is very unlikely that any amount of talking or reading could have prepared me for the painful reality that is an integral part of growing into a new way of life.

As is always the case it is in the small things that change is felt most sharply. Those letters demanding attention, the phone messages needing to be returned, the emails to be responded to—all these were no more. These things and so much more had been a constant background reality and at times had been very irksome; all were now missed; their absence unsettled and disturbed, and it hurt.

FACING SUNDAYS

Sundays presented a particular challenge. For the first time for many years, I would be in collar and tie and sitting in the congregation, but where to go? I had always been used to getting up very early and leading worship from 8 a.m. onwards. The local parish church, at the centre of fifteen or more parishes all linked together, had its service at 11 a.m. And so I found myself driving off into the countryside and discovering those places where eucharistic worship took place at 9.30 a.m., the earliest option in the area. What a different thing worship is for congregations.

There were all kinds of surprises in store. I was amazed to find Merbecke still in use and to hear a choral motet sung unaccompanied as an introit from the west end in a small village church. There were other things not so uplifting or inspiring that lay in wait. Quite frankly much was very dispiriting. This was also the point when I realized I would be living in an area with a different ecclesiology from my own. The vestiges of liberal Catholic Anglicanism were to be found in the buildings and service books, but it was being overlaid, if not supplanted, by faux informality and an evangelical style that grated on me. I developed a habit of slipping into a church of my choice just before the service started and slipping away immediately it was over, with luck avoiding any of the usual church "fellowship"—that now near-compulsory "bolt on" to worship that provides the context where those who know one another chatter away, but where those unknown visitors are left skulking by the walls longing for the terrible instant coffee to cool so that it can be drunk and an escape made.

This state of affairs, it has to be said, is no better in cathedrals. The music and the liturgy may be in the vanguard of all that is excellent and can draw people like me from twenty-five miles away, but go alone to the chapter house for coffee after the service; there you will find the real Church of England. The full theology of the peace, so effusively shared in the aisles, is seen in all its glory. The stranger will invariably be left to his or her own devices and the desire to get out as quickly as possible will soon force an exit—usually before any of the four or five clergy needed to conduct the service have arrived, to be engulfed by members of the cathedral's clerical fan club.

It was on Sundays that so much seemed to come into focus and be most painful. The sense of loss; who was I? What was life to be all about now? How was I ever going to manage the emotions of anger, grief, the hurt, the bouts of irrational anxiety and above all the sense of loneliness? These wracked me throughout the six months before I was granted permission to officiate. Making some sense of it all was a challenge. I began by writing reflections on my experiences of worship. These were private, but at least I was able to earth the experiences and the emotions and laugh at life in an Alan Bennett kind of way. But there was more, much more to deal with.

MAKING A LIFE

I have always been single. I grew up in a loving home with parents who had married and had two children before the Second World War. I came along after the war and grew up in the 1950s and swinging 1960s, which were pretty straight-laced in my street. As a child, churchgoing was a given. I sang in the choir at mattins and evensong in the local parish church and went to Sunday school in the afternoon. I left the choir when my voice broke. After confirmation I progressed to early morning communion and a teenage fellowship on Sunday afternoons, with a church youth club, one evening a week, thrown in for good measure. As I moved further into adolescence, I became aware of changes taking place in me and my body. Fairly soon I realized that the other boys were taking an ever larger interest in girls. Why did not I? Slowly it dawned on me that I was not like the others. There was something different. Indeed, there were a number of differences. Most of the others had ditched religion. Most of the others were always wanting to play and became proficient at football or some other sport. Was I the only person not moving on? Was this something that would pass or would I forever be stuck pining for the wrong people and having the wrong ideas?

Armed with some O levels, I left school and started work at sixteen. In 1968, I took a job in London. It was not long before I knew I was certainly not unique—well at least not in ways I had feared I might be. I was not the only person of my orientation after all. I was gay, and so were others. Hurray. Despite making reasonable progress in my job, I kept feeling that I had to sort out a nagging idea that I might have a vocation to the priesthood. I first became aware of a sense of vocation while I was a very young lad. It had persisted throughout my adolescence and in my early twenties I was sponsored to go forward to a selection conference. Sex and matters sexual were definitely not on the agenda. When I arrived at theological college, I realized that once more I was not alone. What I thought ordination might do for this state of affairs I genuinely did not know. In a society that had been hostile to those of my orientation and at a time when any activity would have been illegal, the Church had been somewhere where gentle acceptance was found. From the time of the selection conference until well on into ministry the code of "Do not ask: do not tell" pertained.

The Revd Malcolm Johnson set up a confidential clergy consultation for gay clergy. It was based in London, and gatherings were held twice a year. As a curate I would try to negotiate with my training incumbent to have my day off so that I could attend. Not that he ever knew precisely why I wanted that particular day that week. Like many others, I found the consultation to be a haven of acceptance and affirmation that made ministry far out in the provinces manageable.

The move from assistant curate to incumbent came after eight or more years in orders. It was at this time that I first came across the subtle discrimination only the Church of England can apply. It became apparent that of all the clergy in the diocese who might be considered for a first incumbency only those who had a wife (and preferably children as well) would be considered for a living. Thank goodness there were other bishops and other dioceses who were ready to accept clergy whether they had a spouse or not.

With the passage of time and increased responsibilities as an incumbent, I found that I prioritized other things and did not make time any more to attend the clergy consultation. By my forties I realized that singleness was what life would probably hold for me but got on with the ministry. At that time the idea of seeking out a "significant other" was just too ridiculous to give any serious consideration. Ministry and life in general were in one compartment, sexuality was firmly entombed in another one altogether.

Gradually things changed. Over the years, society—thank goodness— became more accepting and much more open but, sadly, the Church has become a much less comfortable place to be. Life was made more than tolerable by my having a large circle of friends and colleagues, gay and straight, married and single, who were immensely supportive. Some did know quite explicitly that I was and am gay. Others may know, but it has never been a topic of conversation. Of my nieces and nephews, I have only ever told one, though others may have wondered. My siblings may have guessed as may my parents, but "coming out" has never featured in my family life.

The "Higton" motion debated in the General Synod in November 1987 represents a public turning point. The Church has been caught in a trap of its own making ever since. Lambeth Conferences, synods, several reports, and much anguished episcopal hand wringing have not served the Church, its teaching, its pastoral care, to say nothing of its mission to wider society, well at all. I am amazed that there are any gay or lesbian younger ordinands. I am also full of admiration for those whom I have met who will not conceal their sexual orientation and who are determined to be open about their permanent, faithful, and stable commitment to someone else. Whether we call that a partnership, a union, or a marriage matters not a jot. As far as I can see gay or lesbian clerics, whether they are celibate or in single-sex relationships, are just as capable of being foci for unity and of modelling a wholesome Christian way of life as their heterosexual colleagues, and sometimes more so.

Like all clergy I have had many doors opened to me and had the privilege of ministering for most of my time to people who never came to church. In the course of my ministry, there were odd occasions when I helped clergy in neighbouring parishes whose ministry was deemed to be unacceptable by one of their parishioners. Usually it was someone who never went to the church but who, for a reason only known to themselves, did not want the local priest to minister to them. On just one occasion in nearly forty years did I have any difficulty. A very embarrassed funeral director contacted me and informed me that a resident in the parish did not want me to conduct a funeral for the family. When pressed she revealed that the reason given was the family's assumptions about my sexual orientation. That it was correct and that they had hit the "bull's eye" can only have been guesswork on their part. The young married male curate assisting me at the time dealt with the matter.

We now have a very unpleasant state of affairs which I often consider to be rather like a "holiness war", in which the status of same sex relationships is not the real issue at all, but is the presenting symptom for much larger battles. The underlying substantive issues revolve around the true nature of human sexuality, Christian spirituality, and the authority of Scripture. The leaders of some large eclectic churches that contribute vast sums to diocesan funds for ministry and other smaller groups who live out their lives within very particular theological frameworks keep threatening to leave and take their money with them if the Church gives any ground on same sex marriage, especially for clergy. They claim that their stance is thoroughly based on biblical theology. The bishops appear to be incapable of taking them on, or unprepared to, and so blackmail, not a biblically-based virtue, lingers on the back stairs and stalks the corridors of church life.

In the General Synod and elsewhere there are, I suspect, some who are prepared to fight long and very hard to secure a decisive victory. The immediate effect of that would be to remove from women and men who are gay any realistic possibility of ordination if they do not commit to being celibate, whether in a civil partnership or not. Those like myself who have been ordained for years, whether retired or not, will be ever more isolated and possibly alienated to such a degree that we remove ourselves from any involvement with organized religion. The long-term effect of this and other developments that are likely to follow in its train will be to change the Church of England. The Church that embraced a wide range of theologies will become narrower, and the Church whose *raison d'être* was to serve everyone in the communities of England will be transformed into an Assembly of the Elect.

I now realize that the professor at university was right when he wisely advised, "If you have a call to celibacy, join a community. If you are called to marriage, find a wife. If you are gay, find a partner." Though the professor was correct, I doubt very much if anyone working with ordinands would dare to make such a statement today. I did not follow his advice. Now I must live with the consequences and not complain.

Retirement requires a positive outlook if it is to be anything more than an absence of all that has gone before. I decided to make the most of whatever might be before me. There were false starts and wrong turns like an approach to train as an advisor at the Citizens Advice Bureau and thoughts of doing an MA in Art and Theology.

MAKING A LIFE IN THE CHURCH

Once permission to officiate was granted, I immediately contacted the rural dean and the local incumbent. Both responded warmly, and I was gradually integrated into the service schedules across a huge deanery. My role is to fill in the gaps on the Sunday and weekday service rotas and to conduct baptisms, marriages, and funerals as and when required. I have become expert in navigating my way through some very interesting orders of service that stretch the provisions of *Common Worship* to the limits. Throughout I try to model what I saw as a stipendiary priest when I had excellent retired clergy living and helping out in my parish. What a privilege to do what is asked, when invited, to do it to the best of one's ability—and then shut up. Remembering always to keep out of parish politics and clerical intrigue—what is not to like?

Beyond parochial liturgical duties a former colleague from my title parish has inveigled me into being a clergy widow's officer for two of the archdeaconries of the diocese. A task that involves sending out Christmas cards and dealing with one pastoral crisis in two years is not a demanding ministerial load.

One thing that is very hard to cope with is the sense that what little wisdom one may have accrued in the nearly forty years of ministerial experience is now consigned to the lumber room. Among other things, I had trained numbers of curates, mentored ordinands training on non-residential courses, and hosted ordinands who were doing their parish placements as part of their training at residential colleges. I had developed some simple courses for lay ministerial teams, and like every other incumbent, dealt with the complexities of pastoral reorganization and liturgical revision. There is a collection of Lent and Advent courses that could be dusted off and given a second airing. Nothing of this has ever been drawn upon. I may have retired from a particular ministry, but I am still a priest. If ordination is not just about being given a function for a number of years, but is the recognition of a life-long vocation to serve the people of God, how is this to be more fully realized once one retires?

MAKING A LIFE IN THE COMMUNITY

Retirement does offer other opportunities. As I have a member of the family living in the Far East, I did accept an invitation to spend a month travelling in that part of the world. It was when I got home from that adventure that I have to admit I began to enjoy this new way of life. I have since been to France with other members of the family and most recently to North-West Italy to stay with friends who live there. Running alongside these bits of travel, I have explored other interests more rigorously.

I had always had a vague interest in art and things cultural, and a friend suggested that I look out for a branch of NADFAS. When they mentioned this I quipped, "I have no interest in flower arranging." I had confused NADFAS with NAFAS. The National Association of Decorative and Fine Art Societies (NADFAS) has a host of nationally accredited speakers who lecture on a huge range of topics clustering around art, architecture, sculpture, pottery, and much else besides. I discovered that a branch with 200 members meets in the town where I now live. A new world opened up before me.

I made the mistake of going to a monthly lecture wearing my clerical collar. My cover was blown, and I was immediately pounced upon by the chair with the request that I become responsible for church trails for children. (As well as giving members a chance to hear very good lecturers, the organization's national leaders encourage local groups to offer educational opportunities for children and young people in their communities.) I reluctantly agreed. Very soon I found that I had been co-opted on to the local society's committee as the honorary secretary for trails. Creating trails in churches is a fascinating challenge. It is also fun gathering a team of local people to put the thing together and then helping them to set it out to the nationally moderated standard. One unforeseen consequence is that adult members of the congregation end up discovering things about their churches that they had never noticed before. Primary school teachers who are hard pressed and may not be conversant with churches or confident teaching religious education find these trails give them the means of consolidating and extending the curriculum. With several trails now under my belt, a member of our local NADFAS group has invited me to speak at her Deanery Synod. There really is no escaping synodical life after all.

I have always tried to keep my theological reading going, and in several parishes I have been a member of a theological reading group. No such thing exists in this neck of the woods. What I had never done was to give myself enough time to read novels. Now I had time on my hands, I enquired at the local library whether they sponsored any groups. After some time, one was formed, and we meet on a monthly basis to discuss the book we have or should have read. The discussion can be very wide ranging and is usually accompanied by much laughter. It also surprised me that, despite not wearing clerical gear, once the group suspected that I knew something about religious and ethical issues, members would deliberately raise questions of faith or religion touched on in the novel. From this group came another involvement.

I have always been wary of poetry, if not baffled by it. Like Alan Bennett I have always felt it was a world I could not get into. When I mentioned this to one of the members of the book club, she invited me to go along to a poetry group of which she was a member. In fact, she is the *de facto* leader. Again another new world has opened up. I have learnt about the lives of poets, read some of their works, and begun the process of making the connections between them and their world and us and ours. At times it can be challenging, but it is exciting and fulfilling, especially when something or someone unknown or unrecognized comes to light. It is also striking that at most meetings one or other of the members will look to me to answer theological or ecclesiological allusions the poet has made. I have to be on my toes and ready to retrieve some nugget of knowledge laid down in those university days.

Another group that I have joined is a philosophy group. This meets under the auspices of the University of the Third Age. I had studied philosophy as part of my training, but I have to admit it had never been one of my favourite subjects. In truth I think that the first year was not well taught. The gallop through western philosophy in the second year was wearing, and the combat with philosophical problems in the third was exhausting—but I survived. It taught me to be careful with language, to be aware of the non-biblical roots that inform much of our faith and doctrine, and to avoid confusing assertions with statements of fact.

As I am the only member to have any interest in metaphysics and who also has a faith commitment, it makes for an interesting afternoon. I have learnt to deploy my arguments with care, and I have discovered that I can call others' arguments into question as well as show that their suspicion of metaphysics is sometimes misplaced. I have also opened up hardened agnostics and atheists to the necessity of taking theology seriously and demonstrated to them that the Sunday school religion they learnt as children is best left where they learnt it, in the Sunday school. Grown-ups need to engage with grown-up religion. It is much more exciting, much more demanding, and repays rigorous attention. I have thoroughly enjoyed leaving them disconcerted when I have rubbished their ideas about my supposed beliefs. As I have pointed out on several occasions to one participant, a lapsed Roman Catholic, who claims to be an avowed atheist, "You can take the boy out of the Church but you can't take the Church out of the boy." My refusal to conform to his caricatures of religion and to defend the indefensible discombobulates the other members of the group more than a little. What I have thought for a long time seems to hold true. Sunday schools in general and badly taught religious education in school in particular do far more damage than good.

I also believe that my membership of these three groups brings to light the fact that some of the troubles of our mission-orientated Church are of its own making. The Church of England appears to be engaged on a mission to collect "scalps for Jesus". I understand that parochial clergy are not only to be subject to regular appraisal, as I was, but to be assessed on their effectiveness in growing their churches numerically as much as spiritually. As I heard a preacher at an ordination say at the end of an otherwise fine sermon, whatever else you may be, "As priests you are entrepreneurs for Christ." By joining three different groups, each made up of a mixture of the lapsed and the non-believers, I have found that there is a readiness to engage with ultimate questions. By refusing to trade in glib answers, to deal in assertive biblicism, or hand down "churchy" solutions, I have won some respect for religious claims and now am given a fair hearing. I am in no doubt, few if any of the people I have met are going to become pillars of their local churches, but I think that they may now be a little less dismissive of the faith. Indeed, if I thought it would not cause outrage among churchgoers and chapelgoers in the community, I would really like to set up a group where people who have left the church in all its denominational forms, and who think that they have put matters of faith behind them—the free spirits, the sceptical seekers, and the out-and-out non-religious—could sit and do some theology. The group could be called, "I do not believe it. So why should you? Theology for non-believers." Perhaps this is what I should be doing with my retirement. It would certainly be a bit more fun than many a church meeting I have had to endure, and who knows, might do a little bit of good.

12. THE PRIEST AS NIGHT-SOIL MAN: REFLECTING ON OUTSIDEDNESS

David Peel

I grew up in a suburb of Newcastle upon Tyne with a churchgoing mother who always welcomed my friends to our house—my father died when I was eleven. I was active in my local church, being a server, a member of the parochial church council, and a member of the Anglican Young People's Association (AYPA). There were eleven AYPA branches around Tyneside, with others further afield, and eventually I became diocesan president. I had left school with two O levels, and I worked for twelve years in local government, but was encouraged by David Wood, the diocesan youth officer, to believe that I was more able than my school-leaving results suggested.

REFLECTING ON PREPARING FOR ORDAINED MINISTRY

I believed that, while I could be happy doing many things, I could only be content being a priest. I therefore spent 1970 to 1971 full-time at a local college obtaining the A levels I needed in order to qualify for ordination training, for which the Church then accepted me. I was also offered a place at King's College London, to be taken up in 1972. For the first nine months of that year I served voluntarily with Newcastle Family Service

Unit, which did intensive social work with a small number of families in a deprived part of Newcastle.

> Weep
> If you can,
> Weep,
> But do not complain.
> The way chose you—
> And you must be thankful.

These lines from Dag Hammarskjöld's (2006) *Markings* helped to sustain me as I moved towards ordination, and I still value them.

I found the three years at King's, and the more practice-orientated fourth year at its country branch, St Augustine's College, Canterbury, an altogether wonderful experience, and I cannot express enough appreciation of those who contributed there to my preparation for ministry. I left with a theological Associateship of King's College, the AKC, and the 1975 ethics prize, which was a selection of books of my choice. I think that the prize was the result of my having written a first term essay on poverty and hopelessness, which G. R. Dunstan (never Gordon!), the F. D. Maurice Professor of Moral and Social Theology, suggested I submit for publication—it never was published—and a good end-of-third-year exam result.

At King's, Sydney Evans, the Dean, gave each of us a card; mine has become one of my treasures. On it are the marks of a Companion of the Transfiguration; among these are "to contemplate the mystery of the dying and rising of Jesus, his disfiguration and his transfiguration . . .", "to keep August 6 not only as the celebration of the Transfiguration of our Lord but also as the day when men and women in Hiroshima were disfigured by the exploding of the first atomic bomb", and "to draw strength from the hidden companionship of all others who hold themselves by faith in Jesus Christ at the heart of human suffering and redemption, and to invite others to take their life-stand there".

My fourth-year placement was in Her Majesty's Prison Canterbury. While at St Augustine's, the Warden, Anthony Harvey, took several of us to Paris, where I was able to meet the secretary of the French worker-priest movement. Its members' approach was to be "present with the poor". On another occasion, I spent a weekend with the vicar of Tenterden, who in conversation spotted that the importance of what is ordinary was "my thing".

There is a written assertion about priesthood that I have long valued. In it, I take "thanksgiving" as the literal meaning of "eucharist". Ulrich Simon, the Professor of Christian Literature at King's, and my third year tutor, wrote *A Theology of Auschwitz* (his father had been murdered in Auschwitz), and in this he claims of a priest that "it pertains to his office to make eucharist even in hell" (Simon, 1967, p. 128).

While at King's I frequently worshipped on Sunday mornings at the house of the Southwark diocesan missioner, Ivor Smith-Cameron. The first time I went there I was welcomed by one of several residents, a retired anaesthetist; his first words were, "Come in, the house is yours." The weekly Eucharist was usually attended by about three dozen people, mostly middle class, with a wide age range—the local paper boy used to join us when he had finished his round. Afterwards those who wished to stay shared a meal. Acts 2:42 was important—"They devoted themselves to the apostles' teaching and fellowship, to the breaking of bread and the prayers." Ivor used to say that while conventional church life is "centre-periphery"—people coming from where they live to a church building—validity could just as well lie in a model of church life which recognizes the variety of people's circumstances and offers opportunities for worship wherever they are.

At King's, several of us students started publishing a theology magazine called *Feet*. This name summarized our vision of ministering as being to do with the beauty of ordinariness ("How beautiful upon the mountains are the feet of the messenger ... who brings good news," Isaiah 52:7), with what is ordinary, down to earth in people's lives, and of ministering being about movement, and process. We continued publication into the eighties.

REFLECTING ON THE EARLY YEARS IN MINISTRY

I served my title in St Paul's, Whitley Bay parish, in the Diocese of Newcastle. During that period and later I frequently visited Margaret Kane, to talk theology; she was then Theological Consultant on Industrial and Social Affairs to the Bishop of Durham and in the North East. I had earlier arranged for her first book, *Theology in an Industrial Society* (Kane, 1975), to be launched at King's, having already got to know her. After three years I moved to my second curacy, at Tynemouth St John Percy, Percy Main, North Shields. My brief there was to concentrate on Meadow Well, an estate built for slum clearance purposes from 1932 onwards, and one of several distinct districts in a geographically big parish.

Meadow Well has always been a place of poverty. Poverty is lack of power, resulting essentially from lack of money, but intimately and inherently related to financial poverty are emotional, spiritual, educational, housing, cultural, dietary, and aspirational poverty, poverty of employment, heating, clothing, life expectancy, of physical and mental health, of self-esteem; people in poverty are more likely than others to take refuge in drugs and alcohol, with, frequently, associated crime. They live under extremes of stress, and so difficulties in relationships can result in violence. A lasting impression was made on me in my early days by a teenage girl claiming "We're rubbish".

In 1980, North Tyneside Council had hoped to initiate a twenty-four-hour childcare service on Meadow Well and had therefore set aside a block of four houses that were being modernized. However, funding this proved difficult, so the then diocesan social responsibility adviser and the then social services development officer proposed a joint Church–Council project. After many meetings, therefore, on 8 September 1980 the Cedarwood Centre opened its doors, with two workers, one a social worker and teacher and one a nurse, both of whom lived on the premises. They were funded from church sources, while the council provided the building, and what was called the Cedarwood Avenue Centre Trust was registered as a charity. Subsequently volunteers, local and foreign, were engaged.

The Church and social services related to most people only in times of specific need: the Church when there was a funeral or baptism to be done, and for quite short periods; social services when a family had a problem. Cedarwood was there as a presence, more an organism than an organization, and focused on affect rather than effect, relating to people in the ordinariness of their lives, ordinariness which could be quite hellish. On coming down from the Mount of Transfiguration, Jesus got embroiled in the ordinary distress of the epileptic boy and his desperate father (Mark 9:2–27).

After three years, the original workers were replaced by two less experienced, younger people, so in 1984 I ceased being assistant curate and took up the Trust's leadership. In that year I obtained a Certificate in Religious Studies from Manchester University, with a dissertation called *Insider Outside*—"an exploration of life and ministry in an alienated urban community". After another four and a half years, the diocese thought that I had been in what was quite strenuous work for long enough, so I left. This was probably a mistake, as I was working with a developing team of colleagues, so my position should not have been considered in the same light as a vicar's might have been. My replacement was employed from the day after I left. Other employment was in the offing, and eventually I was appointed minister of Killingworth Local Ecumenical Project, on the outskirts of Tyneside. My successor at Cedarwood left after two years, and as no replacement could be found, some local residents, without my knowledge, invited the then bishop to take tea in a Meadow Well pensioner's bungalow. There, he was persuaded to allow me to return, which I duly did, in June 1991, in time for a riot which happened on the estate in September.

By 1993, Meadow Well was in great need of refurbishment, but as houses became empty they had their roofs stripped and the copper work removed by local "entrepreneurs", so eventually most had to be demolished. To fit in with the development plans the Cedarwood building was included among those, so in 1993 we moved to a two-bedroom first-floor flat elsewhere on the estate. Nobody could live there, of course. In 1999, we were able to expand into a former library beneath us, which fortunately extended under our first-floor neighbour. In December 2016, Cedarwood, helped by a grant-making trust, moved to bigger premises nearby.

My belief is that welcome is key to what Cedarwood offers: people need no reason to visit, but when they do they are offered simple, free refreshments, and the opportunity to bear witness to the value of their lives, to use a phrase offered by a longstanding friend. Everyone is accepted, and my picture is of an "open arms" ministry, in the building and elsewhere. Over the years we discovered that it is the workers themselves who do or do not attract Cedarwood users, and it is from the relationships thus formed that many valuable activities can develop.

REFLECTING ON INSTITUTIONS

Institutions, of which Cedarwood is one, cannot love anyone, but they can facilitate the loving which people need from those who work in them, and who can also evoke love from those they serve. The then leader of North Tyneside Council, who had known Cedarwood well for many years, once described the work as loving the unlovable. In the early days a local woman who had many problems and a very low level of self-esteem was taken aback at being hugged by a worker, but soon came to trust her and her colleague. She is dead now, but I have known five generations of her family. Later, a woman colleague went with a party of local women to Magaluf, a resort in Spain sometimes known as "Shagaluf"; there, she was protected by the women from male predators. Another woman colleague, who had lived on the estate for many years, was often the one to whom people went with their financial and other problems involving the authorities. Both were regarded, by different local people, as "mother". A male colleague working with young people fostered a fifteen-year-old boy who had a highly dysfunctional background, and this colleague is now the honorary grandfather of a young woman who at the time of writing has almost completed a degree course. A sixteen-year-old boy complained to a colleague and me, "So what it amounts to is, you love so-and-so more than me." A middle-aged father of several children sometimes kissed me, saying I was the father he had never had—despite my having barred him from the premises for several weeks a number of times for bad behaviour, almost the only person to be so sanctioned. A woman with many troubles said to me once, "You take everyone's sh*t"—the priest as night-soil man?

We realized that we and our more frequent contacts together formed a quasi-family. Latterly in advertising vacancies we stipulated that anyone appointed would have to be able to receive as well as give love. In all this, I cannot stress too greatly the value of team working, with each of four or five of us workers, whether Christian believers or not, nurturing each other and offering our different gifts to others.

For different periods we offered "Meadow Well Worship", or some equivalent. In the early days we held themed discussions, and when we made a quiet room in the original building, we had a weekly Eucharist there. People regarded this room, and a similar one in the newly expanded second building, as being important, using them on the anniversary of a murder, for instance. Some people referred to Cedarwood as their church. For a time, when we only had the flat, we ran well-attended Sunday afternoon services, and later on, when we had more space, badly-attended Sunday morning ones.

Apart from a note on my 1991 licence that Cedarwood was in the parish of Tynemouth St John Percy, I had no formal relationship with the parish church after ceasing to be assistant curate in 1984, though I did, and do, usually attend the church when not officiating elsewhere. I am not sure whether this was advantageous or not to the ministry of the church in the parish. While at Cedarwood I was paid the usual clergy stipend, plus a housing allowance, by the diocese through the Church Commissioners, but employed by the Cedarwood Trust, as it became after we moved. Until sometime in the 1990s, the diocese paid two of us workers, but from then only me. When I retired, the diocese stopped contributing any money. Although I have spent most of my ministry outside the Church of England's structures, I do understand its financial problems. I believe, however, that Cedarwood, its type and vision and therefore the people it serves, have become marginal to the Church's commitment.

A number of "out-of-hours" activities helped to sustain me over the years. I used to attend, with the colleague who lived on the estate, annual meetings of the Worker Church Group (now defunct), made up of priests and others who had "chosen to be wage-workers in industry as an expression of their faith". Neither of us really qualified in those terms, but it was a stimulating privilege to be included. I also attended the annual gathering of British Liberating Theologies Now, and sometimes the summer meetings of the Urban Theology Unit. I have been to Taizé more than a dozen times, and to Iona fewer times, usually driving a minibus full of Meadow Well people.

In 2000, I obtained a Newcastle University MA in Applied Christian Theology, with a dissertation about pastoral care in Meadow Well entitled *Ordinary Glory*, and in 2007, having been funded by the Lord Crewe's Charity to visit Auschwitz, I wrote a paper called "Theodicy and the Night-soil Man". In 2008, I was made an honorary canon of St Nicholas' Cathedral, Newcastle.

REFLECTING ON MINISTRY IN RETIREMENT

I retired in 2012, aged seventy years and six months. I was succeeded by a Roman Catholic layman, whose employment started a week before I left, and since then Cedarwood has gone from strength to strength. I live in my own house, a few minutes from the estate, as I did before I retired.

Several sets of motifs have helped to sustain me over the years. One is the two-fold nature of outsidedness. In the Bible there are examples of what cannot be tolerated being put outside the camp or the city—the waste matter from the sacrificed animals, the scapegoat bearing people's sins, people being crucified or stoned, and in Hebrews 13:13, "Let us then go to him outside the camp and bear the abuse he endured." But there is also good news from outside the city: Jesus heals the man named Legion, who then wants to go with Jesus; but no—"Return to your home, and declare how much God has done for you" (Luke 8:26–39). Church Action on Poverty (CAP) is a campaigning and educational organization, and for some years we hosted a CAP group consisting of Meadow Well residents and people from two middle class Tyneside suburbs, and we observed good news given by some perceived as society's outsiders to those more comfortably on the inside. And Cedarwood itself was in some ways an outsider, certainly in Church terms, with those of us who worked there leading something of a liminal life.

Another set of motifs of value to me relates to being around. I believe that ministering should be more process than project, so phrases which resonate strongly with me include "I sat where they sat" (Ezekiel 3:15 (AV)); the French worker priests' principle of being present with the poor; the idea of loitering with (good) intent; and a remark, I think by Austin Farrer, in a sermon at another priest's funeral, to the effect that the deceased priest had had the gift of "leaving himself about the place".

I also value John 10:10—"I came that they may have life, and have it abundantly." Alongside this are some words of Irenaeus, Bishop of Lyons (who died around AD 200): "The glory of God is a living man" (see Kirk, 1932, p. 1), paraphrased as "The glory of God is someone fully alive." In this context, we sometimes see the glory of ordinariness, ordinary glory, while recognizing that all living is a process of becoming, of moving towards death and whatever may follow. Part of Ben Okri's poem *Mental Fight* touches on this:

> Every moment thus carries
> The monumental in the ordinary,
> Transcending the political
> Hinting at the evolutionary. (Okri, 1999, p. 16)

For me, Isaiah 42:3 represents the pastoral and political response to these motifs: "a bruised reed he will not break, and a dimly burning wick he will not quench; he will faithfully bring forth justice." Also, I have long tried to remember, in an increasingly unjust society, Amos 5:24—"let justice roll down like waters, and righteousness like an ever-flowing stream", said by Ulrich Simon to be the most important verse in the Old Testament.

And so to retirement. I have been careful not to interfere in Cedarwood's life, while being grateful to my successor for saying, on my leaving, "Don't be a stranger here." Not having had to move house, I have been able to continue some work that I did before I retired, and to take up several new activities. The former include being a member of North Tyneside Citizens Advice Bureau's Board (I am currently chair), and of the Phoenix Detached Youth Project's Board, in North Shields; after I retired I joined the Board of Kids Kabin in Newcastle, a children's project. Before I retired, I did a course in faith accompaniment (a term I prefer to "spiritual direction"), and in relation to that now see two people occasionally. I have long been a member of Church Action on Poverty North East (CAPNE) and am currently chair of the group. Having developed an interest in prisons and the people who live in them, I remain in touch with and visit several long-term acquaintances who are in prison, and the occasional new one. I have continued officiating when requested on Sunday mornings, now virtually every week, and very occasionally at funerals. I have become the "priest companion" to a vicar in Newcastle, and help in her parish roughly every other Sunday and on one other day per week.

I have long enjoyed socializing with friends, but among new activities, I have become the representative for the twenty-eight retired clergy of my deanery, being a transmitter of information, occasional visitor, and organizer of occasional events; I have joined a theology discussion group; and I have become a duty chaplain at St Nicholas' Cathedral, for two hours per week. I do a certain amount of pastoral caring, among other things acquiring thereby increased knowledge of mental ill-health from a woman in hospital with whom I am in frequent contact. My relationships with some members of the Cedarwood "family" have continued, and I have been present at two deaths since I retired. About two years ago I became branch secretary of my local ward Labour Party. And it was good in March 2015 to begin a sermon, "As a priest in the Church of England who happens to have been born gay . . . "—this was at Northern Lights Metropolitan Community Church (NLMCC), which I had been attending since the previous June on Sunday evenings.

REFLECTING ON RETIREMENT ACTIVITIES

I shall expand a bit on three of my activities. First, my involvement with prisons, resumed without pre-meditation from my Canterbury experience: over the years many Cedarwood contacts were incarcerated, and therefore wanted me to visit them, especially if their families were unable or unwilling to do so. Sometimes, particularly with the younger ones, I would take their friends to see them. At present, I am in touch with six imprisoned Cedarwood contacts, and with two others who have come my way. Most of the Cedarwood ones are serving long sentences for quite serious crimes; all these had difficult childhoods—one was in twenty care placements in about six years—and keeping in touch and visiting (and sending in the odd postal order) is a way of being alongside a few of the most excluded of people. With CAPNE members and others I have helped to organize two seminars and a conference concerning prison life, and we are currently planning a scheme whereby we hope volunteers will be supported in befriending a few people in prison who have no one else. Two principles lie behind this: "There is no *they* who go to prison, only some of *us*", and "Nobody should be judged by the worst thing he or she has done." The same "Prison Matters" group has prepared and, when asked to do so, led a two-session course introducing church people to our penal system. A motif in all this is Jesus' saying, "Inasmuch as you visited, or did not visit, the least of my brethren in prison, you visited, or did not visit, me" (Matthew 25:31–46, NKJV). One supposed reason for sending people to prison is that they might be rehabilitated; as with the rest of pastoral care, a deeper understanding of people's need is that they might be redeemed—liberated at a price, as the then Bishop of Newcastle put it when lecturing on *Faith in the City* (Archbishop of Canterbury's Commission on Urban Priority Areas, 1985).

Secondly, the cathedral chaplaincy: the task is to "loiter with intent", being available to anyone who visits the church. People talk about their lives, their problems, where they have come from, seek prayers. Once a young man and his girlfriend rushed into the building, he a little the worse for wear from the previous night out, but demanding an immediate blessing; I managed to discover his name, blessed him, and the pair rushed off. I remember that when I am outside a hostel where people with alcohol problems live, and where I am sometimes asked to say a prayer or to bless someone—an example of the Church being wanted in the variety of people's ordinary circumstances. At the cathedral, I once met a woman who said she had no religion, but who was very familiar with church services. I mentioned that for all the assertions we make about God, nothing can be proved and that for me the idea of God beyond what we think of as God was important—the idea of pure being, the point of mystery where the different religions meet, and where faith and science meet. I was surprised and disappointed when she said that she had never before heard a member of the clergy say such a thing.

Thirdly, Northern Lights Metropolitan Community Church (NLMCC): I have been worshipping there almost every Sunday evening since June 2014, and I preach there once a month; the sermon quoted above was my first NLMCC one. The international Metropolitan Community Church (MCC) was founded to cater for people who are gay, transgendered, or otherwise perceived as sexually "different". Great emphasis is put on the equal value of everyone, upon God's love for all. This is important to those people who have been repelled by other churches because of their sexuality or sexual identity. I find it a very congenial place to be. I have never deliberately been "out" in Church of England circles, and have never been personally victimized. I do think, though, that the official strictures on what gay clergy may and may not do are grossly impertinent, and that the Church presents a repulsive public face to anyone who is gay—though I recognize that many local churches are most welcoming.

The MCC has an open table policy: at each service it is said that "this is God's table, not ours", so anyone is welcome to take communion, whether or not a member of MCC or any other church, provided he or she is seeking a relationship with God. It is also important that non-alcoholic wine is used, so that anyone can participate. Sometimes the minister presides, sometimes one of several lay people.

REFLECTING ON THE CHURCH OF ENGLAND

It strikes me that the Church of England's usefulness varies from place to place, and that wherever it is not of some use in a disfigured world it has gone seriously wrong. I am not keen on the current evangelism fad: it boils down to increasing the size of congregations, often for financial purposes, which I do not think is the best way of being "among you as one who serves" (Luke 22:27). Evangelism can replace service of a community with saving people from their community—and to that extent is anti-incarnational. As the Archdeacon of Northumberland has put it, in support of small churches and not criticizing evangelism, a satsuma is not a failed orange: it has its own identity and quality, and is easier to get into than most oranges.

The Church at every level has to act as an institution, with all an institution's legal rights and responsibilities. But it is not primarily an organization, easily assumed to be the case by people who are good at running organizations. It is primarily an organism—an easy concept to grasp, given our emphasis on being the Body of Christ.

That being so, I think welcome is key to what the Church ought to be giving people. But welcome to what? First, people should be welcomed into whatever helps to serve their real needs—in a non-judgemental atmosphere and a reasonably comfortable, informal setting. Secondly, people should be welcomed into the possibility of experiencing situations that are new to them and which can therefore nurture growth. Thirdly, people should be welcomed into the task of transfiguring a disfigured world, perhaps using the insights of liberation theology, based on God's gratuitous love for everyone. Fourthly, in many circumstances, people should be welcomed to the possibility of worshipping—but worshipping in a way that honours their culture and experience, that avoids presenting a banal version of the faith, with water turned not into wine but "diluted Pepsi-Cola, slightly sweet and good for the kiddies", as Ulrich Simon put it in the first edition of *Feet* (1975, p. 3). Church of England services are middle-class-orientated, and so I think that imagination and flexibility are needed when trying to serve the needs of the likes of Meadow Well people. Constructive opportunities abound for worship to take place away from churches, and where people are more comfortable, culturally and physically; but the worship needs to touch people's hearts and minds. And a few people worshipping somewhere other than in a church should not be thought of as being in transit to the real thing: their bit of Church is fully Church.

There are two Last Supper commands: the synoptic—"Bless bread and wine; eat and drink my body, my blood; do this in remembrance of me", and the Johannine—"Follow my example and wash each other's feet." In the first, the great focus, reminder, and sustainer of everyday thanksgiving, we align ourselves with Jesus and let his life be in us in the ordinariness of our lives. In the second, we are given a part in Jesus' life of service, by being of service to others—by working to transfigure this disfigured world.

I think that both the substance and the practice of these Last Supper commands could be better valued and understood were the receiving of communion open to all. Jesus did not stipulate that participants should be confirmed, and if, as the Church teaches, the Eucharist is a really valuable sacramental gift, surely it should be a gift for all. People who are already excluded from much of society should not be excluded from receiving this gift. We can think also of the prodigal son's father, welcoming the boy with a party, no questions asked (Luke 15:11–24).

There seems to be no New Testament reason why only ordained priests should be allowed to preside at the Eucharist. Writing forty years ago, Anthony Harvey (1975) made this point in *Priest or President?* Even then there was a looming shortage of clergy and lay people were doing more to sustain church life than formerly, so provided the need for church order was satisfied there seemed to be no reason why an authorized lay person should not preside in the absence of a priest. At NLMCC, there is no less a sense of holiness when a lay person rather than the minister presides (although the minister, of course, has not been ordained by a bishop, so we are not quite comparing like with like). And it seems odd that priests are trained over several years to break the Word, but only fully qualify once they are ordained to break the Bread—for which little training is needed. It is not only priests who can preside in washing the world's feet; why the difference when it comes to making Thanks?

I think that apophatic spirituality, which acknowledges God beyond God, God beyond our assertions, pure mystery, ought to be known about by Church people, especially in the light of increasing knowledge of the billions of galaxies, and of humans' (including Jesus') genetic make-up and physical relationship with the rest of creation. In this context, the title of David Wood's (2004) *Dark Prayer: When all words fail* reflects contemporary needs. And I think that in the light of much injustice and suffering, and of the risk of our destroying our home through global warming, the Church should look outwards to the needs of the rest of creation and act with integrity and vigour on what it sees. "Let justice . . . "

Much good work is done, but if we are to be of future use in our disintegrating society, in our disfigured world, Church people must do some creative thinking, starting with three basic questions: who are we?

What may we hope? What should we do? And we should encourage all and sundry to join in. I think God can stand a bit of democracy.

REFERENCES

Archbishop of Canterbury's Commission on Urban Priority Areas (1985), *Faith in the City: A Call for Action by Church and Nation*, London: Church House Publishing.

Hammarskjöld, D. (2006), *Markings*, New York: Penguin Random House.

Harvey, A. E. (1975), *Priest or President?*, London: SPCK.

Kane, M. (1975), *Theology in an Industrial Society*, London: SCM Press.

Kirk, K. E. (1932), *The Vision of God*, London: Longmans, Green and Co.

Okri, B. (1999), *Mental Fight*, London: Phoenix House.

Simon, U. E. (1967), *A Theology of Auschwitz*, London: Victor Gollancz.

Simon, U. E. (1975), "Turning wine into water", *Feet* 1, p. 3–8.

Wood, D. (2004), *Dark Prayer: When All Words Fail*, Harlech: Cairns Publications.

13. WE SHALL NOT CEASE FROM EXPLORATION

Nancy Johnson

When I was asked to write this chapter, my first thoughts were that I would have little to contribute. My experience of ordained ministry, and therefore of retirement, has been very different from that of someone who was ordained in his twenties (it will still be men who have clocked up forty years of ordained ministry) and has served in parish or related ministry for his whole working life. I was ordained in my fifties, within ten years of the first ordinations of women. However, it is probably true to say that I have been involved in working for the church, in one capacity or another, for the whole of my adult life.

EXPLORATION IN MINISTRY

I trained at a Church of England Training College, Sarum St Michael, to be a secondary-school teacher of what we then called "divinity". I wrote my thesis on the "religious life" and spent a great deal of time during my student days in and out of convents. Unlike today, the religious life was flourishing, with plenty of vocations. After two years of teaching, I entered the novitiate of The Sisters of The Love of God in Oxford. This was a silent, enclosed order whose mother superior was the inspirational Mother Mary Clare. It was probably the most formative experience of my early life. We lived mostly in silence and got up in the night to sing the office. There was no escaping the demands of community life or its rhythms of prayer, study, and work. There was no going for a walk, retail therapy, cups of coffee with friends, or any other of the myriad ways we find to distract ourselves in ordinary life. It was an intensive, and not always easy time, but one for which I will always be grateful. If I could have stayed for about three years as Buddhists do, I would have done so. I realized, relatively early on, that this was not where I was meant to be for the rest of my life, and it would have been dishonest to stay and to take even limited vows. So I left the convent and returned to teaching. I remain in touch with the community and have valued their wisdom and prayers ever since.

I went to teach at Grey Coat Hospital in Westminster with its close links to Westminster Abbey. I had lunch every week with the Cowley Fathers and lived in a vicarage in the East End where Trevor Huddleston was a frequent visitor. I worshipped with the West London student chaplaincy, which met in Imperial College in Kensington, and was led by Canon Ivor Smith-Cameron. I mention all this because after my marriage and our move to Sheffield, we attended our local parish church, which was a very different experience. I missed being at the centre of things and spending time with people for whom discussion of theological issues was an everyday experience. In the parish, I dutifully served on the parochial church council, the Deanery Synod, and the Diocesan Synod, and ran the youth club as well as running some house groups. After a few years, and a house move, we became members of an Anglo-Catholic city-centre church which had a gathered congregation and was very different from our previous suburban parish. Here, there were none of the usual parish clubs and societies but a wonderful community of people focused on prayer, pilgrimage, and hospitality.

During this time, I did an MA in Women's Studies and realized just how patriarchal the Church was seen to be. Women's ordination was still years away, so I did my thesis on attitudes to the ordination of women to the priesthood. This was particularly interesting to me as a member of an Anglo-Catholic church, in which there was a variety of views on the subject.

Over the years, we long-term fostered three children and had five of our own. When they were old enough, I went back to work, part-time, in various roles within the diocese, in social responsibility and adult education. Aids was becoming a real concern at the time. A close friend, a parish priest, contracted the disease and despite hostility from the press and some parts of the diocese, the senior staff were very supportive. I spent a lot of time with him and members of his parish, and he died much loved and cared for by his parishioners. I worked in parishes as a diocesan officer and as the bishop's advisor on issues of sexuality, and I was a member of the Board for Faith and Justice. I also did some teaching of parenting classes and domestic violence training. For several years, I worked for a charity based at Church House, working with divorcing couples and children struggling with parental separation and stepfamilies. The charity was founded with a great deal of help from the then archdeacon, Stephen Lowe, who felt that the language the Church used about divorce was unremittingly negative. We spoke of "failed" marriages, of marriage "breakdown", and of children as being products of "broken" marriages. None of this was very helpful, so we sought to help those who were in that situation to see a positive way forward. I worked with small groups of children in schools and did some teacher training sessions as part of this work, to enable teachers to be aware of what the pupils they were teaching might be feeling and experiencing at home.

We moved to worship at the cathedral after a change of clergy resulted in our parish church passing Resolutions A and B. I became a member of the serving team there. With the support and encouragement of the dean, Michael Sadgrove, and the archdeacon, Stephen Lowe, and with many misgivings on my part, I went forward for selection for ordination. I trained for non-stipendiary ministry with the Northern Ordination Course and did an MA in theology. My family was very supportive, but I was aware that my enthusiasm for the venture was less than wholehearted. I served my curacy at Sheffield Cathedral. Michael Sadgrove was a wonderful training incumbent, but he became Dean of Durham halfway through my curacy, and it was difficult for the rest of the staff to have me to train along with everything else. During that time, I was offered a few days of hospital chaplaincy. I had spent some time with the chaplaincy team during my ordination training, as I did my thesis on the care of the dying. I knew I had no vocation to parish ministry, and in a short time it became very clear to me that working in the hospital was where I was meant to be.

There was one difficult conversation with a senior member of the diocesan staff, who shall be nameless, when he said I was a servant of the Church and should go where I was sent. I replied that I was a servant of God, and that it was not necessarily the same thing. I spent the whole of my ministry thereafter as a part-time hospital chaplain. At first, I was in a large teaching hospital, so my duties included some Sunday services and night-time on call. During the last five years of my working life, I was working in a specialist spinal injuries unit. Patients there, many of whom were young men with sporting injuries, have suffered catastrophic and life-changing injuries, requiring long stays in hospital and a completely changed way of life to accommodate their varying degrees of paralysis. Because the unit was a regional centre, patients were often hundreds of miles away from home, from their families and friends. Almost all came from a non-faith background but were forced by their circumstances to ask deeply spiritual questions, about their identity, purpose, and value. I got to know them and the staff on the unit very well, and one of the hardest things about retirement was to say goodbye to them and entrust them to others.

During this time, I was paid by the NHS and worked with an inspirational team of wise and caring chaplains. Like most chaplains, my work precluded involvement in clergy chapters and such like. Few chaplains take a regular part in parish life and tend to be on the edge of church life generally. Working ecumenically, for a secular organization, it is the NHS to which chaplains are accountable, although as Anglicans we have to be approved and licensed by the Church.

EXPLORATION IN RETIREMENT

So, all this preamble is really to say that when I retired, aged sixty-four, I had none of the issues which many clergy face. I continued to live with my husband in the house we have lived in for over twenty-five years, and to see and enjoy the company of my friends locally, whom I have known since we had small children together. Few of them are churchgoers, although they have all been extremely supportive of me. My husband was a civil servant, so has a reasonable pension, and we do not have significant money worries (other than having five adult children who do). We continue to worship at the cathedral when we are in Sheffield, and I take the very occasional midweek service there. I have resisted taking on any helping out in parishes. Partly, this is because I do not feel in any way called or equipped to do so. I can count on my fingers the number of baptisms of healthy children, weddings, and funerals of older people I have conducted, and most of those have been of family and friends. On the other hand, I have done dozens of funerals for stillborn babies and baptized many children at the point of death. Baptizing a child who is not expected to live for more than a few hours at most is very different from a happy family occasion with its promises and hopes for the future of most baptisms. The liturgy has to take account of the situation. While few of the young parents have any background of faith, there is often a real desire to know that their child is safe in the arms of a loving God, even if they are both confused and angry with the God in whom they are not sure they believe anyway. It is neither the time nor the place to ask them for a profession of faith. The faith which the chaplain has can reassure them and maybe bring some comfort.

Taking Sunday services has not been a significant part of my ministry and I never enjoyed preaching, so I do not want to start now. I have nothing but respect and admiration for clergy who continue to work in parishes well into retirement and am aware that many churches could not survive without their generosity, their time, and the benefit of their wisdom and experience. Given that I knew I was not going to be able to offer this, I left it to the bishop to decide whether to renew my permission to officiate. He felt that in view of my ongoing responsibilities at the hospital, it was appropriate to renew it.

So, what was retirement going to mean for me? First, I was determined to spend time with the family. Only one of my children lives locally; one lives in Cape Verde in West Africa, one lives in Tokyo, and two live in London. We have grandchildren in Cape Verde and London, and it is important to me that we spend time with them. The other main part of retirement for me was to spend much more time in my native Cornwall, where we have a holiday chalet. Since retirement, we have aimed to be there for most of the summer each year. Very occasionally I celebrate a weekday Eucharist in the church where I was confirmed. This, of course, precludes any regular involvement or responsibilities in church life in Sheffield. However, as I retired, I was asked if I would do some locum work, as and when I was available, at the local hospice and the children's hospital. I was very glad to do this as I like and respect the chaplains there and value being part of their life and ministry.

At the children's hospital, I cover on-call about one weekend a month and do some regular formal supervision with the chaplain. Supervision is enormously important in chaplaincy as may be imagined. Often chaplains are working in highly charged emotional situations, where families are facing the darkest days of their lives. The serious illness or death of a child can never be treated as routine, or just all in a day's work. Having been a chaplain, it is an area where I felt I could make a contribution to support those who are on the front line as it were. Supervision is a space where the chaplain can, in complete confidence, share and offload some of the effects of such demanding work on themselves as people who are parents themselves. Cases can be talked through and dilemmas shared so that, hopefully, the chaplain can feel cared for.

At weekends on-call, I am not often called out but, when I am, it is urgent and important. As an on-call chaplain I go into situations where I do not know the families. Sometimes, they know the regular chaplain and understandably want a familiar face in a crisis. It helps that I can assure them that I will let the chaplain know about the situation and will ensure my visit is followed up. Handing over to others, trusting that they can do all that is necessary, is an important part of the letting go for me. Sometimes, in the case of the sudden death of a child for example, the time I spend with the family is all there is; I am painfully aware that this day will be imprinted on their memory, and that every word that I say will be remembered forever.

There are occasions when the medical staff need some support too. In the children's hospital this is especially true when there is a case of non-accidental injury, or the death of a child who has been a long-term patient, for example. Again, this is something which will be ongoing for the full-time chaplains. At the hospice I do some on-call and the occasional mid-week Eucharist when the chaplain is away. The chaplains there are very understanding about the fact that I am often away and cannot help.

For me, retirement has been primarily about handing over responsibilities to others. All my life, as an eldest child, I have undertaken responsibilities, in churches, in schools, and wherever else I have found myself. I have had enough committees, and conferences, to last me a lifetime. So, learning to say no, and not feeling guilty about it, has been important. I am not indispensable, however much it has felt like it sometimes. Looking back over my life in the church, of which ordained ministry has been a part, I am not sure that it has always been conducive to spiritual growth. I have always been very busy, and I have enjoyed almost every part of it, but my time in the convent taught me how easy and how seductive it is to be validated by activity.

TIME AND SPACE TO BE

Time and space to be is what I am looking for in my later years. I have been very fortunate in that I enjoy good health, and I do not want to be too busy to enjoy the freedom that retirement offers. My husband and I have done a significant amount of travelling since we retired. We have undertaken two long trips to Australia, visited Sri Lanka, and made annual visits to Cape Verde, as well as shorter breaks in Europe. A few days in Venice most years has been enriching. Spending time in places and with people who nourish me is important. Reading, and deepening my understanding of what it means to be human, to be a Cornishwoman, a Christian, and a priest, in this part of the twenty-first century is part of the task. I am often asked when I am in Cornwall, when I am coming home. It is an interesting question. I have not lived full-time in Cornwall since I was eighteen. Yet, it is still home in a very real sense. I have been reflecting on who I am now, an Anglican priest who has lived and worked in Yorkshire for over forty years, and where I began, as the daughter of a Methodist lay preacher in a Cornish village. It has been quite a journey.

Wisdom used to be associated with the elderly, and now that I am seventy, I feel it is about time I acquired some. Putting aside public office, becoming an anonymous old lady, learning again how to be free, to play, to see things afresh is the way I want to go. In this my grandchildren are a great gift. Parenthood was a joy for me, and it lasted a long time, as I was forty-six when I had my youngest child, but being a grandmother is such a blessing. I love seeing my sons as fathers, and being part of their family lives is enormously important to me. Spending time with small children, listening to them, seeing the world through their eyes is indeed a way to wisdom: "unless ye become like a little child". And perhaps, by spending time back in Cornwall, on the beaches where I spent my childhood, I am reconnecting with the child I once was, with little to do but play in the rock pools and swim in the sea.

I am grateful to the dean emeritus of Durham Cathedral, Michael Sadgrove, who was my training incumbent, for his insight into the connection between "retreat" and "retirement" in his blog northernwoolgatherer.blogspot.co.uk. In the blog for Sunday 9 February 2016 entitled "Not busy in Lent", Michael's reflections on his recent experience of retirement have been a rich source of inspiration for me.

Freedom from responsibility does not mean that there is not real work to be done. Facing old age, with all that that entails, is not for the faint-hearted. I am keenly aware that the future will hold significant losses. There will inevitably be a physical decline. For me, my slight hearing loss is the first sign of this. There will be bereavements as friends and family die and I will have to learn to live with loss. Learning to face up to this with courage and faith is one of the tasks ahead, not just for the ordained, but for all of us. That is why it is increasingly important to me to be clear about what really matters, and what I need to stay with, and what I can let go. At the moment, I can have it all. I can travel between Sheffield and Cornwall easily without a problem. I can go to see my far-flung children relatively easily. It will not always be so straightforward, so I am quite deliberately making the most of my freedom now.

I am still working on what place churchgoing has in all this. In Cornwall, it is the midweek said Eucharists that I attend, and in Sheffield, the Sunday sung Eucharist. I do know that "eucharist", giving thanks, is paramount. I have been extraordinarily blessed in the people who have loved me into life. Wise and holy men and women have given me more than I could ever have dreamed of. Their patience and encouragement, their example, and their belief in me, are not something I ever want to take for granted. I am currently learning so much from those who are older than me, about how they face the future with faith and hope. I feel that spending time on this "soul work" is important and a useful corollary to the play which is also a part of it. The stripping away of public office, status, and being at the centre of things has a monastic feel about it. Who am I, when I am not able to say, "I am a chaplain"? I will always be a priest of course, but I do not want to spend my retirement saying "I used to be . . . ". I hope I can let go enough to be confident and alive enough to grow in other ways.

I have been retired for six years now and feel I have only just begun to understand what it might be about. Talk to me in ten years' time, if I am still around, and I might have cracked it. But maybe not. The journey of faith continues.

14. BEING POSITIVE AND REALISTIC

Pat Robson

I am starting my chapter while sitting in the back seat of a taxi taking me from Cornwall to Luton Airport, which is a very appropriate way for me to start and quite indicative of my rather busy retirement lifestyle. First, however, I need to begin by reflecting on my pre-retirement experience of life and ministry.

LIFE AND MINISTRY BEFORE RETIREMENT

I was married once and had a son, but, because of my health problems, I was unable to have any more children, and my husband and I adopted a three-year-old from Dr Barnardo's. Unfortunately, we were divorced soon afterwards, and I moved to Cornwall with the boys and a huge Airedale and took up a teaching post at a boys' grammar school. In 1987, when I was ordained deacon, I moved to Truro to take up the post of youth officer for the diocese, and three years later I took over the running of a large country parish. During this time, I became guardian to three West Indian children, and a little later I adopted two Romanian children. Three years ago, when I was seventy-two, I adopted another Romanian boy just before his eighteenth birthday. So in all I have had eight children to care for and to plan for throughout my time in ministry and retirement. The first rectory was a joy. It was old and dilapidated and nothing the children could do could make it worse, and it was next to a churchyard so all the neighbours were dead and could not complain about the noise.

There were many times when I felt glad that I did not have to explain the children's behaviour to an angry husband, but there were many more times when I would have liked to have someone with whom to share the ups and downs. Being single is not always as carefree as it sometimes seems to outsiders. And I do have to admit to feeling a bit jealous of my single male colleagues, who were often given casseroles or cakes by sympathetic female parishioners. I would have loved to have come home to the rectory after two or three busy morning services to find a hot casserole discreetly placed on my front doorstep. Perhaps my parishioners thought my children were old enough to do the cooking for me. Some hope.

Now, in retirement, I do not have a husband to do things with or to share these last years. I do, however, have eight youngish people whom I continue to help out as a sounding block, a banker, a taxi service, a filler-in of forms, a babysitter, and a shoulder to cry on. They are all living meaningful lives, and I am very proud of them, but most of them originally came to me with hurts and problems which have never truly been resolved, and I worry for their future. Now in my old age I question my impulse to give them all a home. They may have been much better if they had been brought up in homes where each could have received more individual attention. Still, it is a bit late to think like that and, at the time, nobody was offering. All I can say is that Christmas lunch in this house is a truly ecumenical event and requires everybody to have the patience of saints. It has become an experience not to be missed, and because everyone has made a particular role his or her own, it runs like clockwork. I am always exhausted at the end, but regardless of whatever is happening in their lives the kids always go overboard to make it a day to be remembered, and they always do the washing up.

Just having young people around opens our eyes to modern ways of thinking, which is not a bad thing. Of course, the old ways of doing things will always stay with us and old values will always be the first that come to mind, but we can learn a lot from the young. I think it is important to remind ourselves that they are journeying into a world that we will never know and their opinions and their thought processes will determine the way ahead.

When one of my adopted children confided in me that he thought he was gay, I surprised myself in being quite sanguine about it. He was obviously gentle and effeminate and everything seemed to fall into place. Thinking about it, I felt that he could have a good life as a gay person, that society had become more tolerant and that he had a good chance of finding love and being happy. I was happy for him and began helping him plan his new life. The family, too, were accepting and sympathetic. Over a year later, he came to me again and this time he said that being gay was not right for him after all. He wanted to be a woman. This time we all were a bit shocked. Not because it was what he wanted, but because none of us had any experience of this world and we did not know how or what to think.

He was taking us into a world that was unknown, and, because it was unknown, we were fearful for him. We all of us voiced these fears to him and to each other. We felt that society was not ready to be as accepting of him as a transgender person as they would be if he was just gay. We were afraid he would be considered a joke and would be bullied and ridiculed, and that his life would be miserable. He wanted to change his name, grow his hair and dress as a woman, and we were all worried for him and felt a bit uncomfortable about it all. But he has done all these things now, and he has done them well. Slowly, one by one, we, his family, have learned to accept, and this Christmas when we all got together, I was delighted to see how easy everyone had become with the situation. And it seems that people with whom he meets each day have shown him every kindness and consideration. Of course, there are those who make fun of him when he is out in the evening dressed as a woman. But these people are usually drunk, and he is accepting of their ignorance. The one thing that worries him is the finding of a regular partner. As he says, if he were gay, there are plenty of other gay men who are looking for a relationship, but it has to be a special sort of person who wants to be with a trans person.

FINDING PAID EMPLOYMENT

Twenty-five years ago, I started a charity working with children in Romania. The charity was intended, at most, to have a life span of approximately five years, but somehow it is still going and still has a significant role to play. It means that I have to visit Romania at least four times a year and, although technically I should have a lot more time in which to do this, I am also retired, so I have much less money to pay for fares and so on. I decided, therefore, that it was necessary to find a very flexible, part-time job.

For the last three years, I have been a self-employed study tutor working with university students based locally in mid-Cornwall. I find the work very rewarding and extremely interesting, but it took me a while to understand the current expectations and requirements of the various colleges and award-granting bodies. All my students are doing different subjects, so I am absorbing a lot of new information; when I finish for the day, I find my head is buzzing with subjects as diverse as the political theories of Karl Marx, the educational theories of Piaget or Maslow, the shutter speeds required to take action photography, the food requirements of animals in captivity, and the motivation behind race riots (and that is just this week).

The students all have a variety of problems which, when assessed, entitle them to extra academic help. Their problems include psychological ones, such as anxiety, depression, and bipolar disorder, as well as physical illnesses and dyslexia. It has been quite eye-opening to see how many difficulties some of the young people have to cope with and how determined they are to overcome these difficulties and to graduate.

I am now seventy-five years old and am probably one of the oldest of the tutors being employed in this way in Cornwall. When I originally contacted the agents about the possibility of work, I fully expected to be rejected because of my age. It was a very pleasant surprise to discover that, not only was my age never mentioned, but I was actively welcomed. Even when I initially found the submitting of hours worked and the scanning of essential paperwork online quite difficult, nobody became impatient or made me feel useless and old-fashioned. As a result, I am delighted to say that in some things I have become quite computer literate, and for other more technical matters I have a twelve-year-old grandson.

I am writing all this because I know how easy it is to believe that, just because we are no longer receiving a stipend and have officially retired, our useful working lives have come to an end. For many years we have held responsible, demanding posts in the middle of busy communities and then, suddenly, it all stops. Of course, we are often tired at that point, but, after a few weeks' rest, it becomes very obvious that many clergy are definitely not ready for retirement. Popes are not generally elected until they are in their seventies because the Roman Catholic Church wants a leader at the peak of his experience and wisdom. On the other hand, by the time we clergy in the Church of England reach our seventies we have been put out to grass.

I am sure that some of you reading this will say that retirement was the best thing that ever happened to you; others (including me) will have been only too glad not to have to cope with PCC meetings anymore, but still, there is the niggling thought that never really goes away, that we were called to be priests and that that was a calling to a lifetime of commitment, and was not just a job which stops when the salary stops.

MINISTRY IN RETIREMENT

I am convinced that there is still a real role for retired clergy to play in the life of the Church, and that these clergy should be far more actively involved in the work of the diocese and in the parishes. Of course, the younger clergy must be allowed to steer the Church in new directions without being held back by those of us who have had our day, but while they are steering and dealing with the finance and the politics, the older priests could be well employed just being priests and being known in the smaller communities as someone who will listen and pray. There are hundreds of small communities, many with small, under-used churches that would welcome the opportunity of having an elderly priest among them for a few years; someone who would minister to their spiritual needs while the parishioners took it upon themselves to care for them in return. Logistically, however, clergy tend to retire to places near to larger towns which means that the parishes who need them most are some distance away. Caring for the priest in this case could mean driving to pick him/her up, or providing a small residence in the village. I believe that most retired clergy would welcome an opportunity to continue working in this way, assisting a busy rector or rural dean while doing their best not to interfere in any way.

The number of retired, active ordained clergy and non-stipendiary priests now exceeds the number of stipendiary ordained clergy, and most of us fill in and take services where needed, but it is very haphazard and an incompetent use of man/woman power. If retiring clergy were interviewed before disappearing into the land of the forgotten, to find out what, if anything, they would like to do with their retirement years, the Church could build on their experience and knowledge and all would benefit. Apart from being community or village priests, retired clergy could also be used as advisors, mentors, and spiritual directors. As younger stipendiary priests are given heavier and heavier workloads, often combining a diocesan post with a large number of parishes, there is an even greater need for them to be given support. And who is more qualified to give this support than someone who has already got the t-shirt?

KEEPING ABREAST OF CHANGE

Divorce was unusual when I was growing up; unmarried couples living together were frowned on; having a child out of wedlock was shameful; people with learning disabilities were locked away out of sight; and gay people frequently went to prison. The world has changed. Over the years, our pastoral care work has taken us into the homes and lives of people who have suffered badly because of these old prejudices and doing so has very likely forced us, despite our own childhood's engrained set of values, to see situations in a different light and made us more understanding.

If we are hoping to be of use in a pastoral or counselling situation we need to keep up to date. The Church has a reputation for being old-fashioned and, although we do not need to compromise on values and beliefs, we do need to be seen to be understanding. It is important that we know what is going on in the world, even if we find some things distasteful. It is important, too, to know what is expected of us by way of training and regulations. If we want to be useful, we need to attend the courses that are required nowadays to safeguard our children and our vulnerable adults. As far as the general public is concerned, the Church needs to be seen to put its house in order. I am told that many retired clergy are not happy about attending these three-hour courses on the grounds that they have been working in their parishes for so long that it is like teaching a grandmother to suck eggs. By refusing to attend, those clergy do themselves a great disservice. We are none of us too old to learn, and if we avoid these things it gives others the opportunity to wonder why. The sessions are certainly not intellectually demanding, and you do not necessarily learn very much, but by just being in the group you can share some of your experiences and listen to others who have important things to contribute. In that way, everyone comes away with new, interesting ideas and information as well as the necessary certificate to say they have attended.

Keeping our brains active is also important. When our bodies let us down, we do not want to be bumbling old cabbages unable to hold an intelligent, informed conversation. Our local further education colleges have an enormous number of evening and daytime classes which cover a multitude of subjects. Just browsing through their prospectuses is exciting enough. Those of you who do not fancy going out of an evening could consider an Open University course. Your parish experience alone is usually sufficient qualification to get you on to any degree course, and understanding how to use a computer can be learnt in many ways. Quite often there are very local courses run by people in your own village or by local councils, and these are advertised in parish magazines or in local papers. And if you do not fancy learning you could consider teaching or writing. Your memoirs could be fun, but be careful what you say about the organist and do not make your characters too identifiable. Writing about a topic which interests you would certainly keep you occupied and, if you find a publisher interested in taking it on, it gives you a real thrill. Holding your own published book in your hand is a very special feeling and makes all the hard work worthwhile, but do not expect to make any real money by being an author, unless, that is, you can manage to produce another *Fifty Shades of Grey*.

Another area of interest to those of us who are retired but who still feel we would like to make some sort of contribution in society is in the world of charities. This is something dear to my heart. My fellow trustees and I have been involved in our charity for twenty-five years, and we are concerned for the future. One by one we will drop off our perches, and then the work of our charity will come to an end, unless young, dynamic people get involved or unless we are able to raise enough money to set in place a profit-making enterprise which will make our work self-supporting. We are looking at both options, and so, I am reliably informed, are most charities. Ideas-people and fund-raisers are vital to keep these charities going. People are desperately needed who can write letters, talk, persuade, and plan. Clergy would be ideal. Why not offer your services? Hands-on help is needed as well. One of my boys volunteers every Wednesday afternoon to help with Shooting for the Blind. The mind boggles at the thought, but he really loves doing it because the clients are so appreciative. Many of us have interests or would like to foster new interests, and charities would be thrilled if we became involved in what they are trying to do. If you decide to do hands-on work do not be offended if you are asked to be DBS checked. It is a requirement we should be used to by now.

DEALING WITH ILLNESS

As I know only too well, one of the biggest problems we have to face as we grow older is that our health often lets us down. We have been so busy looking after others that we have often neglected to look after ourselves. As a result, even though they are not actually dropping off, bits are beginning not to work properly, and, if bits are aching, it makes us feel old and miserable. I am home again from my trip to Romania, and my ankle is hurting every time I move, because I have torn some ligaments. I am told it will take weeks to heal, and I feel very frustrated as I am staggering around like a very old lady. The only good thing to come out of this discomfort is that it has forced me to sit down and try and finish this chapter.

Being ill is not new to me. I have had to have several operations for cancer, and each time the healing has taken longer. Luckily, each time the surgeon has removed the problem, and I have never had to experience the terrible business of chemotherapy treatment. The doctors and nurses have been amazing, and I have a high regard for the standard of their care. My parishioners have also been amazing, and each time they have done their very best to help me through to recovery. I am, however, very aware that as I get still older the chances of becoming ill again are very high. I should, therefore, learn to pace myself, but I find this is definitely something I am not very good at doing. If something needs doing, I tend to do it regardless of how I am feeling.

By acknowledging this problem in myself, I am aware that many of us force ourselves to do things when we do not actually feel up to it. Most of us in retirement now were children during, or just after, the war. That was a time when the work ethic was very demanding. There was always something that we should be doing, or someone we should be helping. It became part of us, so that now it is quite hard to sit and relax without thinking of something that needs to be done. Many of us find a holiday sunbathing on a beach almost unbearable because of the terrible feeling of guilt this wonderful laziness produces in us. No wonder we cannot cope with retirement: we are conditioned not to do so.

All this of course is leading up to the obvious observation that retired clergy need counselling and mentoring just as much as the younger, more active ones. The burdens are different, but they exist all the same. I am guessing that many retired clergy may find the services of an individual counsellor a bit galling. What I think they would find more constructive and enjoyable is the frequent opportunity to meet each other socially in comfortable homes or pubs, where one can enjoy a real laugh and a good, old-fashioned gossip. Clergy have lived in the centre of communities for long periods, and what people do and say is of vital interest. Clergy love to gossip, and clergy are smart enough to learn from each other. They do not need to be told by a well-meaning counsellor that perhaps they should try and get out more; they are perfectly able to decide this for themselves, especially if an old colleague mentions that he walks the dog each day and it makes him feel physically fit, or that he has joined a rambling club and talks about the fun he has on the walks. Exchanges of people's different experiences in retirement, a bit of gossip about what is going on in the diocese, a comfortable armchair, and a crackling log fire will make even the most miserable old retiree feel good. And if occasionally the diocese would just let him know that he is respected and his services are essential to the smooth running of the Church, retirement itself would be a joy.

For myself, the luxury I have chosen to indulge in to brighten up my retirement is continuing to take people on pilgrimage to the Holy Land. I have done this off and on ever since I was a teacher in the 1960s and 1970s. I love trying to make the Bible stories come alive for people and try my hardest to make each trip a "trip of a lifetime". It does not always work out just right, but it has done so often enough for me to get a real buzz out of it. So this is my retirement luxury, and I will try and do it for as long as possible. I hope my torn ligaments heal properly, otherwise I might need to find another more sedentary pleasure.

I love these words of the medieval Persian poet, Muslih ud-Din Saadi:

> If of thy mortal goods thou art bereft,
> And from thy slender store two loaves alone are left
> Sell one, and with the dole,
> Buy hyacinths to feed thy soul.

I feel it is important for us all to have a luxury, obsession, or interest of some sort to cheer up the dull days. It is likely to be reading or painting, perhaps gardening or walking or being with family or friends or (dare I mention it?) playing with trains, both real and toy. We all need something to look forward to and make us feel good. We need something to lift our hearts and feed our souls, especially on the wet, gloomy days.

PREPARING FOR DEATH

Before I fall off my perch, I have a few things I want to do. People nowadays call them bucket wishes, and their bucket is usually filled with colourful, exciting things that they have always dreamt of doing. My bucket has a few of these colourful things in it, like visiting India and winning the lottery, but I have a fair number of more mundane wishes and ones that will require my presence in this world for a little longer. Obviously, I hope that the charity that takes up so much of my time is in a position where it can run without my help. I also would like to see all my children happily employed and in loving relationships, but I suspect that is in God's hands and not mine. I would like to have left enough money to pay for my grandson's university tuition when the time comes. I would like my Romanian rescue dog to be calm and well-behaved enough for people to love him enough to want to take him on, and I would like to be able to face death without being frightened.

I recently had the privilege of spending time with a lovely, gentle man who knew he was facing imminent death and who very calmly set about putting his house in order; when the moment came, he departed this life with a smile on his face. This is my most important bucket wish. At the moment, I put the possibility of death very firmly out of mind. A few years ago, I heard that a clergyman I hugely respected had been terribly afraid of dying, and that when his time came, he had desperately tried to cling on to life. His death had been a desperate agony and distressing to his family. I want my death to be serene. I want a good death. I do not want to be afraid, and so I know I must prepare carefully. This takes me back to what I was saying about retired clergy needing counselling. Many of us are probably in the position of having outlived our spiritual directors and have never got round to finding someone new. Probably some of us are spiritual directors to younger priests. I suggested that retired clergy need the company of other clergy in social gatherings, and I still think this is so, but I also think that we may need the help of someone who cannot be fooled by wily old clergy who are adept at avoiding the subject. If that person is one of the younger clergy, so be it. We may not have the option of time, and we may not have too long to procrastinate. A young, sharp-minded clergy person may be just what we need. Illnesses and accidents have a habit of happening when they are least expected, and we have to manage the best we can. My cancer operations have always been in a hurry, and so I have a packed hospital bag at the ready in my chest of drawers.

I had my last stint of cancer six years ago, while I was working in a parish as a house-for-duty priest. This time I picked up a hospital infection, and it was many months before I was able to walk more than a few steps at a time. I could not live on my own in the vicarage, and so I handed in my notice and my eldest son offered me a home with him. He had an old cottage and managed to convert one end into a small place for me. All of this was unexpected, and it took just over two years for me to recover my strength and to want to get back into harness again. That is when I started to look for my part-time job. I needed to help out with the household expenses, and I needed to pay my son back for the loan he took out when he converted his cottage. The unexpected can prove to be very expensive. I still live with my son, and at the moment it suits us very well, but this might not have been the case. We all need to be aware that when we get ill the lives of family members are affected, and we need to plan, if we can, to minimize the problems that might occur. Retirement itself also affects the family and especially the partners, many of whom married teachers or business people and did not originally choose to have parsons as their partners. Some have found it very difficult and can often see retirement as a chance to lead the kind of life they would have liked to lead without parish constraints, and retired clergy often feel that it is only fair that this should be so. Many clergy couples have also sensibly made their plans for retirement and could not be happier.

We are all different and the way we live our lives is unique to ourselves, and, however we do it, it is still important to find a contentment and satisfaction in what we are doing. We can be very difficult to live with if we are discontented, for a discontented person can make those close to them very unhappy indeed. We all need to make the effort to go out and buy those hyacinths.

15.   HOMECOMING

Anthony Phillips

I have never been an incumbent. Instead my ministry has been academic with a strong pastoral element, one which in the end always took priority. But when I offered myself for selection for ordination, I never envisaged that it would end as it did. Indeed, had anyone suggested that I would teach at both Cambridge and Oxford and then even more strangely become headmaster of the school which puts St Augustine as the first of its benefactors, like Sarah I would have laughed outright. But if I have learnt anything in this life, it is that God is a God of surprises.

I was born in Falmouth, though from seven to seventeen boarded at two schools in Devon, in neither of which was I considered a success by the school's standards. Sport was more important than academic achievement, and I was not a sportsman. But my one debt to my secondary school was the headmaster's insistence that in the sixth form we should all engage in public speaking—something which has stood me in good stead throughout my life.

My father regarded universities as dens of vice—ironic given my later career—so at seventeen I left school and entered articles in a Falmouth solicitors' firm. Qualifying five years later, and conscious that my experience of life was very limited, I joined a long-established London firm specializing in trust work. It acted for many landed estates, and Burke's *Peerage* was our bible.

FINDING A VOCATION

I am a once-born Christian. I have never known a time when I did not
believe in God and have always enjoyed worship. As I suspect with
most priests, a combination of influences led me to seek ordination.
My Cornish background was low church, and initially in London I
worshipped in a well-known evangelical church. But I fell out with the
curate whose understanding of the God I worshipped did not square
with my experience. I then gravitated to my local parish church, St
Philip's, Earls Court Road, where there was an interregnum. The church
was largely being run by a splendid parish worker, and the younger
members of the congregation were encouraged to play a full part in
church activities. I taught in Sunday school, took part in a lively Bible
group made up of young professionals, and after evensong on Sundays
with others helped to provide a cooked supper for anyone who cared to
drop into the church hall, mainly elderly ladies and young Australians.

Increasingly I began to recognize that I could have a much deeper
pastoral relationship with people as a priest than I could ever properly
have as a solicitor. The decisive event was meeting on holiday three
trainee Scottish Congregationalist ministers who were the first people
seriously to discuss theology with me. Until then it had never dawned
on me to question the veracity of the Scriptures. Through them I was
introduced to Bonhoeffer's *Letters and Papers from Prison* (Bonhoeffer,
1969) and that decided me on applying for ordination. Throughout my
life, whenever my spirits are low, I have returned to this masterpiece and
drawn renewed strength from it.

I had no degree, so was sent to King's College, London, then staffed
by a plenitude of the country's leading theologians. It was the early
1960s, the time of *Honest to God* (Robinson, 1963). I had never felt more
excited in my life. The dean of the college was Sydney Evans, one of
the unsung heroes of the Church of England. He trusted his men even
when at times there was little reason to trust. I owe him an immeasurable
debt. I specialized in biblical papers, four Old Testament and three New
Testament. Doctrine and church history took me up to AD 451, but only
in philosophy did I venture further. I had to learn Hebrew and Koine
Greek from scratch. I did well enough to go on to Cambridge to read for

a PhD, where I combined my legal training with my love of the Hebrew Scriptures doing a thesis which was published as *Ancient Israel's Criminal Law* (Phillips, 1970).

SHAPING A MINISTRY

By then it was clear that I would have an academic career. Wisely the Bishop of Ely, who ordained me, made me promise that I would do a full three-year curacy: "The university will want you before then, but you are not to go." They did, and I did not. To prepare for ordination, the bishop sent me off to The College of the Resurrection at Mirfield. Although only there for a term, this experience profoundly influenced my spiritual development, for which I am deeply grateful. I served my title as first curate in a new church on a Cambridge housing estate which earthed my ministry before, as the bishop had predicted, I was appointed to an academic and pastoral post at Trinity Hall, Cambridge.

I was lucky in my time there to do a considerable amount of television and radio work. I loved making programmes, writing scripts, and particularly doing vox pop. I shall always remember watching myself on television, with my young son on my lap mystified as to how I could be in two places at once. Although television had more excitement and glamour whether in the studio or out filming, I preferred radio which, relying on words alone, could explore theological issues in much more depth. After five years as a don at Cambridge, I moved to a similar role at St John's College, Oxford.

My first President at St John's was the medieval historian, Sir Richard Southern. He had an amazing rapport with the undergraduates—too close in view of some of the Fellows. Single-handed he took the college from near bottom of the Norrington table to the top, near which it has remained ever since. A devout churchman, he was daily at mattins in the college chapel. I was later to model my headmastership on him.

Throughout my time at Oxbridge, I taught the Old Testament but was also responsible for the pastoral welfare of the whole college community. Colleges are like families, and every member matters whatever their role. Indeed, at Oxford I particularly relished being appointed domestic bursar, though my other office as steward of high table nearly ended in disaster after I had served for dinner frogs' legs.

In my late forties and having done roughly the same job for fifteen years, I wondered what I should do next. Teaching in Oxbridge is done largely by tutorials for one or two pupils at a time. Much as I enjoyed this intimate interaction with pupils, I wanted to take on a position where I was ultimately responsible for the running of the institution. Mrs Thatcher offered me a deanery, but in a rather acrimonious meeting with her appointments secretary in 10 Downing Street, I turned the offer down. I knew I was not a dean. Like the late Lady Runcie, "too much religion makes me go off pop". To my utter surprise two years later I was headhunted to apply for the headship of The King's School, Canterbury and ultimately even more surprised to be appointed. As one former headmaster pointed out to me, I had no qualifications other than my wife. She had been his secretary.

Knowing my left-wing views, many were surprised that I accepted the post, and I had myself been very uncertain whether it was appropriate for a priest to devote himself to the education of very privileged children. Unlike many of my colleagues, my own children were being educated in state schools. In the end, after consulting many friends who gave me differing advice, I decided that if I was appointed, I would take it though, despite knowing God as a God of surprise, I had no idea if it was what God wanted for me. Indeed, I have long recognized that few can know in advance what is God's will. Mostly we have to act in faith, and it is only by looking back that we can have that faith confirmed. As the then Archdeacon of Oxford put it, "Isn't it better that someone with your views should be headmaster than the usual candidate?" And being a cathedral school, I would have no difficulty in being able to continue to exercise my priestly ministry.

The Headmasters' Conference ran an induction course for new heads. We discussed everybody one could think of connected with the school— even the duties of headmasters' wives though none were present—except the chaplain. Indeed, the only time religion was mentioned was when one very senior retired headmaster pulled his pipe from his mouth and said, "Never let your chaplain hear confessions." I have no idea whether any of mine did.

I was very careful not to trespass on the chaplains' territory and hugely valued their support. The school's chapel for its main services was the cathedral, where I regularly celebrated the Eucharist in the crypt or preached at mattins in the nave. About once a term I did a week's assembly. I also, unusually for a large school, taught an examined paper, Old Testament A level, committing myself to a quarter timetable. With successful results from a mixed ability class, I was able to establish my credentials in an initially suspicious common room. It was this teaching of bright pupils eager to learn that I was to miss more than anything else when I retired.

Many parents were immensely distinguished, some household names. But when talking about their children, they were no different from any other parent. I had the good fortune when I started of having three children aged between eleven and fifteen at another school in Canterbury, though my daughter was to come to King's in the sixth form. So I was not personally isolated from teenage problems and tensions. At one time I consoled a parent that I was the only member of the family not wearing earrings, and in our family males predominated. That my elder son started his degree at a polytechnic was a useful antidote to parents who were overambitious for their child's academic success.

Although the school had a superb pastoral team of housemasters and housemistresses, tutors, chaplains, and a counsellor, inevitably the headmaster finds himself in a pastoral role, whether with parents, pupils, or staff and this cannot be avoided. Obviously, there is a danger of a conflict of interests as the school's ultimate disciplinarian, but today even an expulsion is a pastoral exercise in which the primary concern is the welfare of the pupil. And no school can escape tragedy which may involve pupils, parents, or staff—often causing excruciating pain within the community. My very last act as headmaster was to visit the bereaved parents of a sixth-form pupil killed in a car crash yards from his own home.

FINDING MINISTRY IN RETIREMENT

Appointed at fifty, my contract was for ten years. So at sixty I retired. I had rather assumed that with my academic record—a fistful of publications behind me—and the experience of successfully running a multi-million pound business, the Church might find some post in which I could exercise further ministry. But, in spite of lobbying by some influential clerical friends, that was not to be. Perhaps turning down Mrs Thatcher had its consequences. But even twenty years ago liberal academics were regarded with suspicion, let alone headmasters of independent schools. So we left Canterbury for the small Cornish village of Flushing, across the Penryn river from my native Falmouth.

Ecclesiastically I already had a position in the Diocese of Truro, as for many years I had been canon theologian occupying a stall in the cathedral and supporting the bishop in a variety of ways, from lecturing to clergy to looking over the bishop's House of Lords forthcoming speech. We had also been regular visitors to Cornwall for family holidays and, living in a tied house, we bought as our first matrimonial home a holiday cottage on the Lizard. As a result, we got to know a number of priests in the diocese who were kind enough to use me for occasional preachments.

Flushing itself was joined with another village, Mylor, where, when we arrived, the incumbent lived. Inevitably living in Flushing, I got to know the local community well, participating in all sorts of village activities. As a result, I was often asked to take an occasional service—baptism, marriage, or funeral. Always I insisted that those who asked me should first obtain the incumbent's permission, which was always generously given. When, nearly twenty years later, we left the village and a party was given for us, as I looked round a room filled with about eighty people, there were very few for whom I had not officiated on some occasion. From time to time I took some of the regular services and also ran a Bible group.

Outside the parish, I was frequently asked to preach, did some academic lecturing, and started to take pilgrimages to the Middle East, as well as lecture on cruise ships. Although no one could fail to enjoy the luxury of the latter, it was actually the land tours which gave me most pleasure, particularly in introducing pilgrims to the biblical lands of Israel, Palestine, Jordan, and Syria. Later my pilgrimages would go to countries such as Armenia, Georgia, and Ethiopia, home to the oldest Christian churches. Retirement also gave my wife and myself the opportunity to travel further afield particularly with sons in the States and a sister in Australia.

I was happy to take up particular appointments. So for some years I served as chaplain to the Order of St John in Cornwall and chaplain to a group known as the Homecomers, Cornish men and women who like myself had worked outside the county, but returned usually in retirement. In addition to being canon theologian, for a brief two years I was one of the original chapter canons, and along with one of the residentiary canons helped to compose the first cathedral statutes.

Before retirement, I had played a part in the wider church. I was an examining chaplain to four bishops and for two years Archbishop of Canterbury and York's Interfaith Consultant for Judaism, which on one occasion took me to Rome and a private audience with the Pope. I was also briefly a member of the World Council of Churches Consultation on the Church and Jewish people. While at Oxford I had stood for the university seat on General Synod, but lost by one vote to Garry Bennett, twenty to nineteen. At the time I went to Canterbury, I was asked to join the Doctrine Commission, but with so much new to learn as headmaster, felt I could not accept, which I now regret. In retirement I served as a senior selector for those seeking ordination but resented the requirement to enquire into the sexual orientation of candidates, which I ignored. Sadly, the hypocrisy of the church over gay issues continues to its huge detriment.

Obviously, education continued to be an important factor in my life. I was delighted to serve twice as a governor of a local further education college and also as a governor of two independent schools in Dorset. Retirement also gave me the opportunity to write, and although my serious academic career ended when I went to Canterbury, I have been able to complete a number of "popular" theological books as well as collect my academic articles on Biblical Law into a single volume. Some, but by no means all, of my books were published by SPCK on whose Board I sat for many years, becoming chair of publishing. I am a regular reviewer for the *Church Times*.

TAKING UP NEW INTERESTS IN RETIREMENT

But retirement should give one the opportunity to take up new interests. For me it was the art world. Despite being brought up only a short distance from St Ives, I knew very little of the Cornish artists until I went to Cambridge to study for my doctorate and became a friend of Jim Ede at Kettle's Yard.

Jim used to lend undergraduates and graduates priceless works of art from his collection, noting what had been borrowed in pencil in an exercise book. As far as I know he never lost anything. So I had works by both Christopher Wood and Winifred Nicholson in my room in college. Besides introducing me to artists like Ben Nicholson, Christopher Wood, Alfred Wallis, and Gaudier Brzeska, he also loved to talk theology. Every evening he would ring the angelus at St Peter's Church. Jim opened my eyes to my Cornish heritage, which in retirement I was able to embrace.

At Canterbury other important influences were the potter Geoffrey Whiting and the artist John Ward. And later in Cornwall, I relished the friendship of Michael Finn. I was to use his crucifixes in a book I published on the seven last words from the cross, which had earlier been the subject of a three hours devotion one Good Friday at Truro Cathedral. Michael was himself to die on that day of crosses just before the book was published.

What I learnt from these artists was a different form of spirituality from anything I had hitherto found within the more orthodox boundaries of the Church. While Michael was a devout Catholic, the others were not orthodox believers. But for all of them, and there were others too, their interest in art in very different forms had an honesty about it which spoke to my deepest needs. Both the visual and the tactile suggested something other, beyond, the mystery that is creation of which we ourselves are part. Becoming even marginally part of this artistic life has prepared me better than anything else for that final journey when I shall meet face-to-face the Creator himself. In my last years in Cornwall, I was to become the representative of the Art Fund in the county.

But what for some years occupied me more than anything else was being involved with the Royal Cornwall Polytechnic Society, a Victorian society founded in Falmouth for the study of arts and sciences and with a very distinguished history, of which I was successively chairman, president, and honorary vice-president. It had inherited a large and valuable collection of the paintings of the Falmouth artist Henry Scott Tuke, which were in a deplorable condition. I managed to raise over £100,000, mostly from outside the county, to have the paintings conserved, framed, and catalogued in a splendid publication. This led to a number of exhibitions, and individual paintings from the collection are regularly being borrowed as the collection gets better known. They are now housed at Falmouth Art Gallery and are a very important part of the town's heritage. It is the proudest achievement of my retirement.

REFLECTING ON RETIREMENT

As my eightieth birthday approached and with both my sons living in the States, my wife and I decided that we should join our only other child, our daughter in Oxford. So it is exile again. It was not an easy decision but a sensible one: all of us, however unwillingly, need to make sensible decisions not only for our own benefit but for the benefit of our families too. I am delighted that almost on arrival, the High Sheriff, whom I married to her husband many years ago, asked me to be her chaplain.

What then have I learnt in these last twenty years of retirement? First, to accept that one is retired. Like most priests I found it hard: giving up one's recognized ministry is bereavement and one simply has to live that out. Without title, office, or employment we inevitably feel non-persons, useless in an ever more frenetic world where what one does defines one. Missing the pupils was the worst of it for me. For five years, until all those whom I had admitted to the school had left, I mourned. Once I knew I would know no one in the school, I relaxed. We are not good at practising what we preach.

Happily, all of us can continue playing some part in the life of the Church. Indeed, increasingly without the support of retired clergy many dioceses would grind to a halt. But too often it has been my experience that priests feel guilt-ridden that they are not doing enough and cling on to an absurdly onerous church routine which dioceses are only too keen to exploit. Retirement should bring a new freedom, an opportunity to do new things, rather than a hanging on. Now is the time quite legitimately to exercise that proper selfishness which in active ministry was rightly impossible to practise. Our families, so often neglected in the past, deserve that.

I am though by no means certain that we should so readily agree to prop up a parish system no longer appropriate for our age and which needs radical reappraisal. Indeed, our willingness to fill the gaps is preventing the Church from facing the real issues of our times as to how ministry can be exercised in a largely secular society where increasingly the parish is a meaningless concept even in rural areas. We cannot go on pretending that the Church of England is a national Church which through the parochial system is responsible for every acre of the land. Indeed, the expense of maintaining both the plant and the hierarchy of every diocese militates against an effective Christian witness however much retired clergy make ends meet.

A more effective ministry for the retired would be to act as mentors. Many of those ordained today have not had the advantage of being academically challenged in a secular university, nor had that rigorous preparation that residential theological colleges provide in preparation for ordination. Dioceses should be ready to draw on the collective wisdom of retired clergy so that all those in active ministry of whatever age could have someone to whom they can turn for advice, as in the old days so many of us had in our spiritual directors. Even apparently such straightforward things like the ordering and conducting of services can be hugely improved with the help of those who have been conducting them for years. How many clergy have been taught how to use their voice as those of us at King's London were by the redoubtable Audrey Bullard? I am now used to being greeted after preaching by members of the congregation whose first comment is that they could hear me. And those who have been academically trained have a duty to challenge both clergy and laity on the theological issues of the day by making themselves available to dioceses and parishes for lecturing and teaching.

But finally—and in many ways more importantly than anything else in retirement—we now have the opportunity to deepen our own faith, and to do that first by quite simply giving thanks for all that has been, however imperfect. God has allowed us the privilege of ministry, a privilege like nothing else on earth. But for most of that time the opportunity for our own spiritual development has been scarce. Retirement gives us time to reflect, read, pray, time to look ahead without any need to justify our daily routine, to look ahead to our own death. It has been said that clergy live such long lives because they are frightened to meet their maker. Well, that will happen and retirement—not given to everyone—gives us the luxury and the space to prepare. And it is my belief that as we do this, paradoxically we shall become more considerate people in the community in which we find ourselves as we exhibit a restfulness, a harmony, a peace within ourselves.

And that being all of a piece will spill over onto all whom we encounter in our daily lives. It will bring a stillness to the frenzy that is all around us. It is this resting in God which can enable others to find God anew through us. In such a way our ministry is completed. To know priests who in their contentment mirror God is a joy beyond words, an encouragement to stretch out oneself to what is beyond, to embrace the otherness of life here and hereafter which no words can describe. In the end it is being rather than doing—something that for much of our working life we ignore—that really matters. And yes, in this holy preparation, God may yet surprise us. For my part, I hope God does.

REFERENCES

Bonhoeffer, D. (1969), *Letters and Papers from Prison*, London: Fontana Books.

Phillips, A. (1970), *Ancient Israel's Criminal Law: A New Approach to the Decalogue*, Oxford: Blackwell.

Robinson, J. (1963), *Honest to God*, London: SCM Press.

16. REFLECTING ON THE NARRATIVES

David S. Walker

The personal stories told in the preceding chapters of this book add up to a rich picture of what it means for a member of the clergy to move into retirement ministry. It is helpful to have such a wide range of both previous ministries and current ones covered, from chaplaincies and sector ministries to parochial posts of all kinds.

By the very nature of the voices heard, they are not intended to provide a complete picture of what happens to clergy after they leave their final substantive post. These are the ones who have chosen to remain very much involved in active ministry of one kind or another. To the extent that they have particular criticisms to make of how the Church treats them, either at the point of retirement or later, they need to be listened to carefully. These individuals may be voicing more gently what others might have put with greater force or acerbity. They are also, by and large, those who have found a way to make this phase, or several phases, of post-retirement work, rewarding and fruitful. Not all will have made the same transitions so effectively. However, putting their stories together allows some important common themes to be discerned and explored, and that is the task of this final chapter.

I am writing this chapter as someone who is still very much in active full-time ministry, albeit now within a decade of retirement, and who exercises oversight of more than a hundred clergy ministering in retirement of one form or another across a diocese. While reflecting on the stories told in this book, inevitably my views are influenced by having seen lots of other good and bad examples over many years.

At the highest level, three broad categories of issues have emerged: the transition into retirement; the nature of a settled ministry post-retirement; and what is distinctive about retirement for (many) clergy. The sections that follow will focus on the transition first, then look at what emerges thereafter. The distinctive nature of the clerical retirement will feature throughout. Where possible, I will suggest ways in which the Church might respond to the messages being given by our contributors.

GETTING OVER THE HUMP

Several contributors referred to the challenge of getting over that initial hump of retiring. Notwithstanding such preparation courses, in which many reported having participated during the immediate preceding years, repeatedly the experience was described as having been harder than anticipated. For many there was a loss of motivation and purpose, a period of tiredness that went on for longer and ran deeper than imagined, and a sense of having gone through some highly supportive and flattering farewells then suddenly "being nobody". While the challenge for those clergy who are also having to move home at this point may have been more acute more often, it would be a mistake to assume that there is not also a huge change for those who have worked outside tied accommodation or even outside the parochial systems. Nor is this purely a factor for those who have been ordained many years. Rather, the loss of holding an overarching role, as the principle means of exercising ordained ministry, presents a huge challenge to many individuals' sense of identity and purpose.

LOSS OF SOCIAL LIFE

A number of contributors reported that a significant challenge was the loss of their social life. Church of England clergy are shown disproportionately to be introverts. This suggests that many will choose the sustaining of existing relationships over the making of new ones. They may also be more comfortable, when they are making new relationships, if they are doing so in situations where they have a clear role, one that carries an expectation of them initiating contacts. The tendency for parochial ministry, both to cover social events and to leave little time for clergy to develop significant outside interests, means that their social lives prior to retirement are often bound up in the social round of the parish and deanery. Moreover, the loss of a social life on retirement is not simply another example of what most will have experienced several times during a ministry that has included a number of moves. The parish to which one retires, especially if a gap is required before the local bishop will consider giving permission to officiate, offers no icebreaker to making new contacts. It may have been many years since the priest was faced with a similar challenge. Furthermore, many clergy will have been used to being able to set up new social events that fit with their own preferences more closely than what might be on offer in the church to which they retire.

BANNED FROM THE PARISH

A number of respondents referred to the practice of not being allowed to return to their former parish to take services on request, or to become a member of the congregation. Most accepted that this is probably a necessary rule, in order to allow the parish to move on and a new minister to have the freedom to take up the role that they themselves have relinquished. Moreover, many may have heard the stories of former incumbents making their successors' lives a misery through repeated interference, even if entirely well intentioned. However, they also recognize and want to put on record the pain this has caused them. For some retiring clergy, the struggle to find another place where they feel they belong in the church is both long and hard. They genuinely believe that they, or at least their spouse, could sit in church week by week and that not be a problem. What is often not recognized is how hard it becomes for the laity in such a situation to offer to their new incumbent the same level of support in making changes that they would give if the predecessor, or someone seen as very close to the predecessor, was not present. Similarly, in the early years of a new ministry, some of the best opportunities for building support from both congregation and wider community come when the new priest officiates at a wedding, funeral, or baptism of someone held in high regard in church or society. Disproportionately these are likely to be people who knew the previous minister well, and where the family would like the former priest to come and lead the service for them. What is encouraging from the stories in this volume is that, notwithstanding some early frustrations, misunderstandings, and sadness, clergy and their families appear to be successful in finding a new congregation where they feel they belong. A more permissive regime for those retiring might bring short-term benefits to them, but the overall cost to the forward movement of the parish and the establishment of the next minister outweighs these benefits.

MONEY AND HOUSING

Parish clergy continue to be one of the few professions outside the public sector for which a Defined Benefit Pension Scheme remains open both to existing members and new ones. However, the cost of retaining a scheme, one which remains highly popular, has been an extension of the number of years required for full service. At the same time, the state pension age has risen a little for men and more significantly for women. It was noticeable how many of those telling their stories felt not just a desire to find some remunerated ministry in retirement, but considered it necessary in order to maintain what they felt to be an acceptable standard of living. It would appear from the clergy in this book that by and large they have been able to find such work. However, the moment of retirement remains a pinch point. Many have enjoyed living in relatively large properties up to that moment, and downsizing is a challenge.

At any one time around 30 per cent of stipendiary clergy require support from the Church of England Pensions Board in order either to rent a property or be helped through shared ownership. Most other clergy will either be able to afford a property or continue in their existing home after retirement. The cohort who have written here are broadly representative of that. Where there has been dependency on the Church to subsidize housing costs, there has sometimes been resentment at the system. This has been particularly evident where changes in rent-setting policies have required a long transition period to keep them cost neutral. Those benefiting from a new policy expect immediate full transition; those who were better off under the previous regime want the longest possible period to adjust. Good customer care, and lots of explanation can help, but the sense of being a recipient of charity, for those who have often been significant contributors in time, talents, and money to charitable ventures, can be galling.

FREED TO SPEAK MORE OPENLY

One repeated comment by some contributors was that in retirement they feel more freedom to speak their own minds on matters. For some, this has allowed them to espouse more radical or more liberal attitudes and opinions, for example, regarding human sexuality, than they felt free to do in office. By and large the opinions expressed as examples of this do not come across as being in any way outside the range of opinion within the Church of England. That would tend to suggest that fear of upsetting members of the local church, and perhaps losing them from the congregation, rather than any fear of annoying those seen in authority over them, is the significant driver for self-censorship. The opportunity to speak out given by retirement is experienced as a perhaps unexpected bonus. While not all opinions so expressed will be welcomed everywhere, the ability and willingness to offer constructive challenge from within the family of the Church is one that ought to be encouraged.

A PARISH OR WIDER RETIREMENT

For some contributors, the ministry they have found in retirement has been very much an extension of parish ministry, but without many of the administrative burdens associated with being the parish priest. They have thrown themselves into pastoral work or become the first port of call for a small church that is part of a wider benefice (what is sometimes referred to as a focal minister). Some describe this as returning to something closer to the form of ministry for which they originally trained. Not all have found this possible, perhaps because the particular benefice to which they have retired does not welcome their contributions at such a level, and no alternative is within an acceptable distance. For others, opportunities have come and gone with changes of parish priest.

Alongside this however, a large number of those who have contributed their stories describe ministries exercised over a much wider terrain, taking on chaplaincies, being given diocesan responsibilities, exercising governance roles within the charity sector, and taking up the mentoring and coaching of younger clergy. Some are remunerated, others offered entirely voluntarily. The range of ministries described, and the obvious sense of fulfilment experienced by those undertaking them, were both more than might have been anticipated. Retirement, for a good number of clergy, would seem to enable a lifting of eyes far beyond the parish boundary, and an enjoyment of having the time to give to such wider roles. Moreover, through the exercise of such ministries, our writers have been enabled to feel very much part still of the wider Church's mission and work, not simply individual and isolated pastors. There is much in the tales told here that should encourage both clergy retiring and those who have such roles in their gift, to consider how the two can best be matched. The current changes to how the Church of England provides oversight and support to those with permission to officiate, both at the point when such permission is first sought and annually thereafter, may well provide more robust mechanisms for identifying gifts and interests.

WISE OR OUT OF DATE

The statistical work at the beginning of this book notes that among those clergy who are at the oldest end of the age spectrum, attitudes espoused are significantly more conservative than among the younger retirees or wider church.

Several chapters mentioned the challenge of being a retired minister in a Church where priorities have changed and moved on. Attitudes however varied widely. Some felt that retired clergy needed more opportunity to call the Church back to a wisdom it was sacrificing in pursuit of the latest trends, and perhaps even synodical clout to give their views greater weight. Others were extremely cautious about becoming unnecessary brakes on the changes the Church needs to make. These clergy prefer to see their role as to accept the current ministerial and missional priorities of present-day leadership as belonging properly to those in charge today. They in turn sought to add their own contribution to the fulfilment of these goals, or to backfill pastoral needs that the current incumbent no longer had the capacity to meet.

Some limited synodical representation for retired clergy does exist, via the capacity to elect one of their number at deanery level, who in turn then is enfranchised for wider elections. It is unlikely that moves to extend this further would be popular, and indeed the desire for it to be done appears to be very much a minority voice among our contributors.

SUPPORT FOR YOUNGER CLERGY

A number of contributors described that one way in which their experience and wisdom were being used was through acting as mentors, coaches, or spiritual directors for other clergy. In some cases, this was simply a matter arranged between the two individuals privately, in other cases it was as a part of a diocesan scheme. Some noted the relatively fast track through part-time training, then a single curacy of around three years, after which stipendiary priests are plunged into leadership in a benefice that may have more churches and complexity than a generation ago. Indeed, many of the posts that might traditionally have been styled as suitable for a first incumbency have been joined to larger benefices or other responsibilities. Moreover, when an apparently "lighter" parish is advertised, graduating curates are often competing with more experienced colleagues, including those seeking a step down in responsibility for a final pre-retirement post. Finally, with later ordinations in recent times, many stipendiary priests may serve only one incumbency before retirement.

All this makes for good territory for the types of personal support related in this book. Some of it clearly requires a considerable degree of trust between mentor and mentee, for example where both are based in the same benefice. Yet, while we only have here the picture from one side of the fence, it would appear that much good work is being done and that dioceses might consider how to set up such (perhaps voluntary) schemes where they are not as yet available.

THE SECOND PHASE AND BEYOND

Our older contributors were able to write of how retirement is not a single moment of shift. Those who had been very active in the first decade or more often described a second, if more gradual, process of setting things down and turning in a different direction. Currently, life and health expectancy statistics suggest that many of those retiring, clergy or otherwise, are likely to have a good decade or more of decent mobility and capability during which they can take on the kinds of new ministries described in many of the earlier chapters. However, the processes of aging catch up with all. Some of the most moving accounts have been the descriptions of setting aside the more outgoing retirement ministries, and a fresh focus both on the immediate pastoral role of the priest, and on the minister being freed for a time of greater spiritual growth. There are descriptions here of preparing for death and what lies beyond it. Those clergy who have written about this process have done so in a positive tone. This change is something to be embraced and accepted. And the time granted to them to prepare for it, especially precious. Not least, after many years of caring for and supporting others, they are finally able to attend to themselves.

CONCLUDING THOUGHTS

The stories told in this volume should provide both a warning and considerable encouragement to clergy contemplating retirement. The warning is that, no matter how much you think you have prepared for it, it will probably come as a shock and take some time to get over. The encouragement is that so many clergy in retirement are exercising fulfilling and important ministries, either to support the local parish and its incumbent or to further the work of the wider church. Those who need to earn during retirement appear able to find part-time work, while others are freed up to volunteer. Their practical skills as well as their wisdom are called upon, and their forbearance in not seeking to remake the Church in the image of a former generation is appreciated.

This book should also be an encouragement to those in positions of responsibility in parishes and dioceses today. There remains an excellent, highly experienced, and motivated cohort of retired clergy among them, who have much to offer that both supports the maintenance of the Church in the present day and also promotes its calling to proclaim the faith "afresh" in every generation. Retired clergy belong to the Church of the future as much as to the Church of the present and to the Church of the past.

This book also draws attention to two areas in need of further research and reflection. First, this volume draws on the experience of clergy who have, mostly, been retired for some time, and have developed patterns of continuing ministry beyond the date at which they started to receive their pensions. Repeatedly, we have heard how it was often not until after the initial shock of retirement had been worked through, that new opportunities were discovered and grasped. While that may be in part because such matters are hard even to consider ahead of retirement, it would also appear that very little support was given to clergy in the years leading up to this point. Pre-retirement courses are largely generic and afford minimal space to explore an individual's particular skills and experiences for future opportunities. It would be very useful to see research conducted with a cohort of clergy pre-retirement, to discover how their "offer" is likely to match with the future Church's "ask", and whether more substantial preparation for ministry after retirement, perhaps including training on particular skills, would both enable a smoother transition and unlock an additional treasure chest of resources for the Church.

Second, while the stories told offer glimpses into how particular clergy locate their ministry within their theology of priesthood, a more focused study would likely produce a much richer resource. The various traditions within Anglicanism ebb and flow in terms of their prevalence in the Church at any one time, and they are also subject to trends and fashions within themselves. Simply to assume that the understanding of priesthood held by those retiring maps neatly onto the understanding of those who will have authority to provide them with space and opportunity to minister would be unwise. Moreover, the journey into and in retirement may, as with other stages of an individual's faith journey, impact significantly on their theology. There is much here that would reward further study.

Lightning Source UK Ltd.
Milton Keynes UK
UKHW021053180920
370087UK00010B/2270